AF712918

Professional Practice in Governance and Public Organizations

"Professional Practice in Governance and Public Organizations" offers cutting-edge insights and practical guidance for professionals in the areas of economics, politics, public policy and public administration, and those working at international organizations. The series features concise and accessible books on the latest developments in governance, organizational and political strategies, institutional policies, policy instruments, public management, and finance. Leadership and digitalization issues are a core topic throughout the series. All volumes are written by practitioners, experts and leading authorities from think tanks, non-governmental organizations, and public and international organizations. While the books are explicitly intended for professionals in the above-mentioned fields, students of economics, political science, public policy and public administration will also benefit from these practical guides for their future careers.

Alexandros Mourmouras • Peter Rangazas

US Economic Policy in the 21st Century

Springer

Alexandros Mourmouras
International Monetary Fund
Washington, DC, USA

Peter Rangazas
Indiana University Indianapolis: IUI
Indiana University
Indianapolis, IN, USA

ISSN 2731-9776 ISSN 2731-9784 (electronic)
Professional Practice in Governance and Public Organizations
ISBN 978-3-031-36436-5 ISBN 978-3-031-36437-2 (eBook)
https://doi.org/10.1007/978-3-031-36437-2

© The Editor(s) (if applicable) and The Author(s), under exclusive license to Springer Nature Switzerland AG 2023
This work is subject to copyright. All rights are solely and exclusively licensed by the Publisher, whether the whole or part of the material is concerned, specifically the rights of translation, reprinting, reuse of illustrations, recitation, broadcasting, reproduction on microfilms or in any other physical way, and transmission or information storage and retrieval, electronic adaptation, computer software, or by similar or dissimilar methodology now known or hereafter developed.
The use of general descriptive names, registered names, trademarks, service marks, etc. in this publication does not imply, even in the absence of a specific statement, that such names are exempt from the relevant protective laws and regulations and therefore free for general use.
The publisher, the authors, and the editors are safe to assume that the advice and information in this book are believed to be true and accurate at the date of publication. Neither the publisher nor the authors or the editors give a warranty, expressed or implied, with respect to the material contained herein or for any errors or omissions that may have been made. The publisher remains neutral with regard to jurisdictional claims in published maps and institutional affiliations.

This Springer imprint is published by the registered company Springer Nature Switzerland AG
The registered company address is: Gewerbestrasse 11, 6330 Cham, Switzerland

Contents

Chapter 1
Twenty-First Century Economics

The USA faces several trends that are the basis for many of its current problems and that significantly threaten living standards into the future. The unfavorable trends are a long-time in the making, beginning in the middle to late twentieth century and worsening during the twenty-first century. Many developed countries face similar challenges, but the problems may be most severe in the USA. Three of the trends are purely economic and are closely related: a fiscal gap in the funding of government obligations, slowing economic growth, and rising income inequality. A fourth trend, global warming from climate change, is perhaps even more of a long-run concern and has both economic causes and consequences. It also has indirect connections to the three purely economic trends.

As with all structural features of a society, the trends are driven by established policies and social conventions. The policies and practices have become the norm over decades and have not been seriously questioned. Flaws in economic policies have contributed to the situation by encouraging current consumption over high-return investments that could help reverse the unfavorable trends and improve economic prospects in the future. This book discusses these flaws and offers suggestions for how policy should be reformed.

Many of the current policy debates are discussions of piecemeal attempts to address what are the *symptoms* of underlying long-run trends. Our view is that it would be more effective to deal directly with root causes. Economic research has identified policy reforms that can eliminate the fiscal crisis, moderate the decline in productivity growth, reduce wage inequality, and mitigate global warming in a consistent and nonconflicting manner. The central unifying issue is how a wealthy society, during the late stages of economic development, achieves an efficient level and allocation of investment in the future.

© The Author(s), under exclusive license to Springer Nature Switzerland AG 2023
A. Mourmouras, P. Rangazas, *US Economic Policy in the 21st Century*,
Professional Practice in Governance and Public Organizations,
https://doi.org/10.1007/978-3-031-36437-2_1

The Fiscal Crisis

Beginning in the 1980s, the federal government of the USA began conducting fiscal policy with spending set consistently in excess of tax revenue. These fiscal *deficits* have been persistent for more than 40 years (with a brief 4-year period of surpluses in the late 1990s) and have caused the government to increasingly rely on bond financing to fund its expenditures. As a result, outstanding government debt has grown faster than output and income in the USA (see Fig. 1.1). The debt-to-GDP ratio was less than 30% in the early 1980s and has recently exceeded 100% (for the first time since WWII). Revenue shortfalls in the large Social Security and Medicare programs, if not addressed, will greatly expand the debt going forward. Under our current spending and tax policies, fiscal deficits will become much larger over the twenty-first century. By century's end, the projected debt-to-GDP ratio is forecasted to be between 300% and 400%.[1]

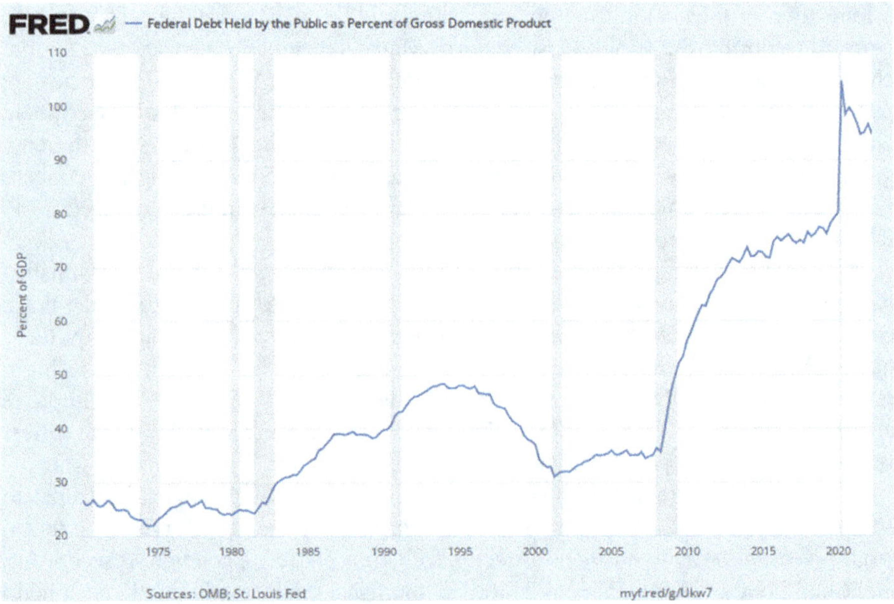

Fig. 1.1 Public debt ratio
Source: U.S. Office of Management and Budget and Federal Reserve Bank of St. Louis, Federal Debt Held by the Public as Percent of Gross Domestic Product [FYGFGDQ188S], retrieved from FRED, Federal Reserve Bank of St. Louis; https://fred.stlouisfed.org/series/FYGFGDQ188S

[1]See the Congressional Budget Office (2021). The numbers are for government debt held by the public rather than total government debt which includes debt held by government agencies such as the Social Security Trust fund. The distinction between the two measures is discussed further in Chap. 2.

Few believe the USA can maintain a policy stance that causes its government debt to reach four times its national income. At anything close to this debt level, the country becomes vulnerable to an increase in interest rates (which would dramatically raise the cost of servicing its debt) or a sharp dip in economic growth (that automatically increases some types of spending and reduces tax collection). Negative events like these increase the chance that a county, even the USA, would be forced to explicitly or implicitly (by government created inflation) default on debt repayments.

As debt levels continue to rise, it will become harder for the USA to find lenders willing to purchase the increasing amounts of new debt issued. At some point, the lenders may no longer look at US government debt as a completely safe store of wealth. The risk of default will cause lenders to require higher interest rates on US debt in compensation. As interest rates rise, lenders' fears become self-fulling because a debt default will be forced by the unmanageable portions of total tax revenue needed to fully service interest payments to bondholders.

The scenario just described is not an abstract possibility. In September 2022, these events played out in the UK despite their current and future fiscal picture being *better* than the USA. Dramatic tax cuts were announced with no associated spending cuts, implying a significant increase in government borrowing. Bondholders, anticipating the higher yields needed to attract new lending, sold their existing debt. Bond prices plummeted and bond yields spiked.

In response to the bond market meltdown, government officials lost their positions, a new fiscal plan with smaller tax cuts and new spending cuts was announced, and the Bank of England intervened by buying the government debt bondholders were selling. Bond-buying completely reversed the Bank's plan to *sell* government bonds to reduce the money supply and the high UK inflation rate. The Bank, at least temporarily, traded off its inflation-fighting stance to restore financial stability.

Is the USA so different that there isn't a lesson to learn? US officials at the Fed and the Treasury department are not at all sure. After the UK bond market crisis, US government factfinders were sent out to quiz Wall Street participants about whether a similar meltdown might happen in the USA (Simialek et al. 2022). The response was that it could but is not likely imminent. They also expressed that their current confidence in the bond market is supported by the belief that the Fed, as the Bank of England, would intervene to quell a bond sell-off. Financial stability would again trump inflation fighting.

A continual rise in the debt-to-GDP ratio over the twenty-first century is unsustainable because it increases, each year, the likelihood of such a bond market crisis. To avert a financial market collapse, the US policy stance must change so as to lower the growth in spending and raise the growth in tax collection, as in the UK.[2] The US fiscal gap between spending and taxes, and the policy reforms needed to close it, are discussed in Chap. 2.

[2] Tajitsu (2022).

Slowing Economic Growth

Worker productivity growth in the USA began to slow in the 1970s. From 1920 to 1970, the average annual growth rate in worker productivity was a robust 2.82%, pushing real wages across the entire income distribution higher. From 1970 to 2014, the growth rate averaged more than a full percentage point lower at 1.62%. From 2015 to the beginning of the pandemic recession in 2020, labor productivity growth averaged less than 1.5%.[3] The majority of the workforce now no longer experiences any gains in real wages over time. In fact, many workers have living standards that are below those of their parents.

The decline in worker productivity growth is related to three phenomena that seem to generally characterize the later stages of development. First, there are diminishing returns associated with marginal increments in physical capital deepening (the provision of more plant and equipment per worker). Second, it becomes more difficult to generate further gains in embodied skills and educational attainment—what economists call diminishing returns to investment in human capital. Third, the rates of investment in physical and human capital per worker decline as more income is devoted to consumption rather than saving and investment. In sum, richer economies devote smaller fractions of their resources to building up capital and receive less future output per dollar invested.

Diminishing Returns

A basic principle in economics is the diminishing marginal productivity associated with increasing any one input in the production process. As one input is increased, relative to other inputs, the additional input tends to be used less intensely and does not increase output as much as past increases that occurred from lower initial levels. This is what happens with *capital deepening*, a rise in physical capital relative to the quality-adjusted workforce used in production. High levels of capital per worker cause low returns to further investment.

As plant and equipment have grown faster than the quality adjusted workforce, the marginal productivity of capital has fallen. This shows up as a secular decline in the average productivity of capital (output per unit of capital or per unit of the capital services from the portion of the capital stock utilized). Morkunaite (2019) shows that the average product of capital has trended downward in richer countries since the 1980s. The diminishing marginal product of capital also reveals itself in falling returns to financial claims on physical capital, such as equities. Rachel and Summers

[3] See Gordon (2016, Figure 1-2) for the period 1920 to 2014 and data from the CEIC on ceicdata.com for the period 2015–2020.

(2019) show that the cyclically adjusted real yield from owning the Standard and Poor's 500 companies has also trended down since the 1980s.[4]

Diminishing returns is associated with the accumulation of human capital as well. The fixed input in this case is the ability and willingness to learn that is established by genetic traits and early childhood experiences. Direct evidence from estimation of human capital production functions that relate education investments to wages and indirect evidence from observing gains in educational attainment both verify that it becomes increasingly difficult for an individual to gain additional skills and for a society to push larger fractions of its population to a given skill level. Despite ever rising real spending per student at the elementary and secondary levels, increases in the average years of schooling have slowed considerably in richer countries. There is also evidence that what is learned from a given year of schooling has fallen off. In fact, many college graduates are paid wages that do not cover the cost of college.

Chapter 3 discusses human capital policy and its connection to economic growth in detail. While diminishing returns is inevitable, there are ways the USA can reallocate its different types of educational investment to raise average worker productivity.

Slowdown in the Rate of Capital Investment

The USA has seen a long-run decline in its net national saving rate. The net national saving rate averaged about 15% of GDP from 1950 to 1975.[5] Since then it has declined significantly. Before the Great Recession of 2008–2009, the net national saving rate was below 4%. The US domestic investment rate has not declined to the same extent as national saving because of an influx of foreign saving. Chapter 4 discusses the persistent trade imbalances caused by US dependence on foreign funding of domestic investment. Despite the foreign funding, the net-of-depreciation *private* domestic investment rate has nevertheless declined significantly, implying a

[4]While the *real earnings yield* has trended down the last 40 years, the *total real return* to stocks, which includes capital gains from rising stock prices, has not. This is because of at least two factors that have driven the demand for stocks and stock prices higher than corporate earnings alone would imply, in other words, stocks have become more attractive for a given earnings stream. First, the transaction cost associated with forming diversified portfolios has been falling. Second, the real interest rates on bonds as a saving alternative to stocks have also been falling. The downward trends in transaction costs and real bond yields have created capital gains in stock prices that roughly offset the decline in earnings and dividend yields. If transaction costs and real bond yields stabilize, these sources of capital gains will disappear and the total real returns to stocks will fall in line with the decline in the real earnings yield. For more on this distinction, see Siegel (2023, Chapter 10). Also note that the real earnings yield is a better proxy for the return to physical capital, while the total real return is more important to an individual financial investor. For example, just because it is cheaper to put together a well-diversified portfolio does not mean that corporate physical capital is more productive.

[5]Kotlikoff (2015, Chart 2).

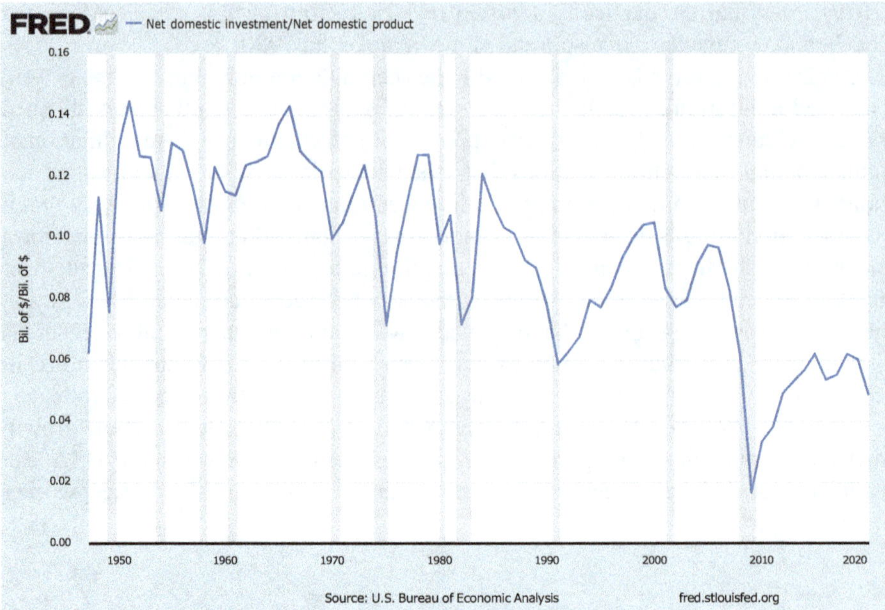

Fig. 1.2 Net domestic investment share of the USA
Sources: U.S. Bureau of Economic Analysis, Net domestic investment: Private [A557RC1Q027SBEA], retrieved from FRED, Federal Reserve Bank of St. Louis; https://fred.stlouisfed.org/series/A557RC1Q027SBEA and U.S. Bureau of Economic Analysis, Net domestic product [A362RC1A027NBEA], retrieved from FRED, Federal Reserve Bank of St. Louis; https://fred.stlouisfed.org/series/A362RC1A027NBEA

smaller annual increment in private physical capital than in the middle of the twentieth century (see Fig. 1.2). *Gross* investment as a fraction of GDP has remained fairly constant. However, because more of our capital stock is small equipment such as computers, rather than large equipment such as manufacturing plants, the annual depreciation rate of the capital stock has trended upward. The country has to now invest more just to maintain its capital stock than was the case in the past.

There has also been a decline in *public* investment. Government infrastructure investment in the USA measured about 3.5% of GDP in 1970. Today, it is about 2.5% and net infrastructure investment is currently only 0.5%. As a result of this decline, the public infrastructure of the USA has depreciated to an embarrassing degree in many locations.[6] At least part of the reason for the fall in infrastructure investment is the growing share of government budgets devoted to subsidizing the consumption of retirees (the primary source of the fiscal crisis) and to repaying principal and interest on debt.

Another important public investment is the financing of basic research. The fraction of federal funding for the basic research, which lays the foundation for

[6]See Friedman and Mandlebaum (2012) and Malinovskaya and Wessel (2017).

technological progress, was cut over the last quarter of the twentieth century.[7] In addition to the same budget pressures that are crowding out public infrastructure investment, there is a concern that individual governments now face reduced incentives to invest in basic research because of the increased ease of international spillovers of knowledge.[8] If each country attempts to free ride off the basic research of other countries, technological progress across the globe will fall. This is why international agreements must take steps to support research and protect property rights, a topic covered in Chap. 4 on international economics policy.

In addition to the neglect of public investment, other aspects of fiscal policy have much to do with the decline in the private investment rates mentioned above. In Chap. 2, we explain how the rapid expansion in Social Security and government debt not only threatens fiscal solvency but also reduces national saving and private investment.

Similar to physical capital, the slower growth in human capital is not only due to diminishing returns but is also caused by declining rates of *investment in learning*. As discussed in Chap. 3, student study time while in college is falling, course content is slipping, and smaller fractions of university budgets are devoted to academics. Investment rates in private capital, public capital, and human capital are all declining in the USA.

Over the last quarter-century, investment has shifted away from physical capital to *intangible capital*—firm-specific ideas, worker training, and business practices.[9] *Intangible investments* are limited by the same forces that limit physical investment. These forces include the availability of funding from saving, the supply of general or portable human skills in the workforce, infrastructure quality, and the general knowledge provided by basic research. In fact, the argument has been made that intangible investment is *more* dependent on public infrastructure investment and human capital investment than the old-style physical capital investment.[10]

Technological Progress to the Rescue?

There is optimism that computer-related technological advances will raise economic growth rates above those of the twentieth century, helping to rescue us both from slow growth and our fiscal problems. However, computer-related technological advances have been with us for some time, including the 50-year period over which economic growth rates have fallen considerably. Computer-driven technological progress has not stimulated economic growth the way earlier twentieth century technological advances did. Moreover, to maintain the current relatively

[7] Vijg (2011).

[8] OECD (2015, pp. 51–52).

[9] See, for example, Haskel and Westlake (2017).

[10] Hazan et al. (2021).

modest growth, new sources of growth will have to be quite dramatic to offset the forces that continue to put downward pressure on growth rates around the developed world.

While some believe we can come up with the new ideas needed to restore growth, a pessimistic view for technological progress going forward is supported by evidence. Charles Jones (2002) relates technological progress to the growth in researchers (scientists and engineers engaged in research and development). In the twentieth century, the growth in researchers was based on population growth and on growth in research intensity (the fraction of the available work force devoted to research). Jones points out that sustainable growth only comes from population growth (as with all investment rates, the fraction of the work force devoted to research is bounded). Assuming population growth remains similar to that of the second half of the twentieth century, long-run growth from the creation of new ideas is expected to be less than ½% per year.

An interesting article in the *Economist* (January 12, 2013), entitled "Innovation Pessimism," lays out some of the issues in the debate over technological progress. The article presents another reason to be pessimistic about growth. There may also be diminishing returns to research and development efforts (which Jones (2002) does not assume). Recent research by Bloom et al. (2017) finds clear diminishing returns to research effort. They conclude that larger and larger increases in research effort will be needed to maintain technological progress at its *current* pace. Vijg (2011) argues that the pace of technological progress will slow, and in fact has already begun to, particularly in the important areas of energy, transportation, and medicine. The article points out that the pessimism about technological progress is contested by those who argue that the growth impact of innovations in computing, biotechnology, and personal communications has not yet been fully realized. Brynjolfsson and McAfee (2014) claim that we are just on the cusp of a second machine-age built around the computer and the development of artificial intelligence.

Another reason to suspect a decline in technological progress in developed countries relates to immigration patterns. While there are international spillovers of knowledge, some of the new ideas generated within a country stay there (especially if they are part of the intangible capital of domestic firms). Rich countries tend to attract high-skilled and entrepreneurial labor from developing countries. Survey studies by Vivek Wadhwa (2012) have revealed the importance of immigration for innovation in the USA. In the USA, only less than 15% of the population is foreign born. However, this relatively small group has contributed about 25% of US global patents. Foreigners, already in or looking to do business in the USA, receive half of US domestic patents. Immigrants are responsible for almost 30% of new business formation, an important determinant of job formation and new products.

Econometric studies provide evidence consistent with the implications of Wadhwa's survey data. Hunt and Gautheir-Loiselle (2010) estimate that a 1 percentage point increase in the immigrant share of US college graduates increases patents per capita by 9–18%. Their estimates suggest that over the 1990s, the 1.3 percentage point increase in the immigrant share of college graduates raised patenting per capita between 12% and 21%.

At US universities, international students make up 74% of graduate electrical engineering students, 72% of computer and information science students, and 50% or more of the students in pharmaceutical sciences, mathematics, and statistics (Alden 2022). Bilgin et al. (2019) find a country's foreign student share has a robust positive association with economic growth in a cross-section of OECD countries despite the presence of several controls for the possibility of reverse causation (from growth to immigration).

As is commonly known, many high-skilled immigrants are from China and India. Wadha sees evidence that high-skilled immigration from Asia into the USA is weakening. The reason is a combination of expanding opportunities in their rapidly growing home countries and the restrictions and delays associated with the US visa process. Alden (2022) notes that more Indian students are now heading to Canada than the USA, a pattern likely to be replicated by Chinese students if the tensions between the USA and China continue to ramp up. Chapter 4 argues that without reform of immigration policy needed to ease entry of high-skilled labor into the USA, there will likely be a decline in our innovation, entrepreneurial activity, and economic growth.

Increasing Income Inequality

Income inequality in the USA has been rising since 1980. Much attention during the rise has focused on the growing income share of a small percentage of households with very high incomes. The top 1% of income earners saw their share double from 10% to around 20% of total income from 1980 to 2000. Since 2000, the income share of the top 1% has remained roughly constant. Much of the income flow in this high-income group comes from the accumulated wealth of older households and does not reflect a pure lifetime measure of the inequality in worker productivity and wages. We think the wage inequality in the bottom 99% of the population is more closely related to the slowdown in economic growth and popular acceptance of the rise in government debt. Coincident with the steady worsening of these two problems, wage inequality has continued to increase after 2000. For these reasons, we focus on wage inequality.

Wage inequality is predominately a sign of education inequality. More educated workers receive higher wages than less educated workers and as the education gap between workers widens, so will the wage gap. The second half of the twentieth century saw *both* a widening education gap *and* skill-bias technological change that created a relatively strong demand for the highly educated, further contributing to rising wage inequality.

From 1950 to 1980, the supply of college graduates increased at about the same pace as the demand for college-educated labor, leaving the relative wage or *skill premium* paid to highly educated labor approximately unchanged. However, as we suggested above, the ability of a country to increase its supply of human capital is eventually subject to diminishing returns. After 1980, increases in the average years of schooling began to slow as the percentage of young workers receiving college degrees stagnated. The demand for college graduates, spurred on by skilled-biased technological change, began to outpace the supply of skilled labor causing the relative wage paid to highly educated workers to increase.

From 1980 to 2005, the wage or skill premium paid to a college graduate over a high school graduate more than doubled. In 1980 a college graduate earned 37% more than a high school graduate. The skill premium rose to 87% by 2005 (Goldin and Katz 2008, p. 95). More recent estimates of the skill premium show little change since the turn of the twenty-first century. In 2015, the estimated premium paid to a college graduate was 90% (Valletta 2018).

A related feature of the USA is the disturbing degree to which one's early childhood experience affects long-run educational attainment. The socioeconomic status of parents is becoming an increasingly important determinant of whether a child graduates from college. Among eighth graders that receive *high* test scores, only 29% graduate from college if their parents are in the bottom socioeconomic quartile, while 74% graduate if their parents are in the top quartile. The importance of parents' college education for household income *and* for the educational attainment of their children implies a lack of economic mobility over generations. As a result, the wage correlation across generations in the same family has become stronger over time.

After 2000, the increase in wage inequality was driven by more than just whether one received a college degree. The rise in wages for many college graduates weakened, while the overall college premium was largely unchanged. Wage inequality *among* college graduates began to grow. The continued rise in overall wage inequality in the twenty-first century has been concentrated *within* the group of college-educated workers (Lemieux 2010). This is known as rising "residual" inequality because it cannot be explained by easily observed characteristics such as differences in years of schooling. More than in the past, high returns to college depend on the *major* chosen and whether the student goes on to *graduate school* or receives *on-the-job training* (which can be quite extensive in many larger firms). Only those with quantitative skills and post-undergraduate education and training are seeing their standards of living grow. College is no longer a good investment for many college graduates, which is one reason that enrollment and graduation rates have stalled.

Chapter 3 explains why the growth in the average years of schooling has slowed and why wage inequality has risen since the 1980s. We argue that a major reallocation of government support for education needs to occur to remedy these problems, an allocation that is less biased toward the minority of the workforce that currently benefits from college.

The troubling US trends associated with the major economic problems of the growing public debt, slowing economic growth, and increasing income inequality are summarized in Table 1.1.

Table 1.1 US economic trends

	Mid-twentieth century	Early twenty-first century
Public debt/GDP	0.3	1.0
Worker productivity growth rate (%)	2.8	1.5
College wage/High school wage	1.4	1.9

Geopolitical Tensions and Globalization

The frustration caused by slowing economic growth and rising income inequality across the developed world has led to populist movements. Frustrated households who do not fully comprehend the reason for economic troubles are susceptible to leaders who scapegoat foreigners as the source of their problems. There is a backlash against globalization from the extreme left and the extreme right, as they compete for votes by both claiming to have the answer of how best to protect the interest of US workers. In Chap. 4, we present evidence showing that international economic activity, including immigration, increases US economic growth without major negative consequences for income inequality. Immigration can also help lessen the fiscal crisis by increasing the population share of younger, taxpaying workers.

The movement toward protectionism and closed borders is aided further by political tensions between the West and dangerous authoritative states in China, Russia, Iran, and North Korea (Roubini 2022). The political tensions not only threaten international trade but also make the essential international cooperation needed to effectively address climate change much harder and could cut off important sources of growth across the globe.

Climate Change

The three economic trends discussed above will lower welfare. A potentially larger and broader threat to the standard of living in the USA may be climate change. It has become increasingly clear that the earth's climate is changing and mostly due to human activity. The effects of climate change on the welfare of future generations are difficult to determine but economists agree that the effects will be significant and will become worse due to government inaction. The problem of climate change and the lack of a prompt policy response to it bears some resemblance to the fiscal crises facing many developed countries. Both problems have been long in the making: decades of greenhouse gas accumulation for climate change and decades of population aging and expanded transfer payments to retirees for the fiscal crisis. In each case, the necessary policy responses will be costly, creating an incentive for politicians to ignore the problems and shift the burden of dealing with them to future generations.

The consequences of greenhouse gas accumulation stem from the warming of the earth's temperature. Projections based on climate models suggest the average surface temperature of the earth will rise between 3 and 7 °F or 1.7 and 4 °C (Emanuel 2012,

p. 53). Some argue that the climate models are likely to be too conservative in their temperature forecasts because they are based on gradual patterns taken from past data. They omit the nonlinear effects of melting ice sheets, disproportionate warming over the poles, and the potential warming effects of *all* the different pollutants that we emit (Wagner and Weitzman 2015, pp. 11–15).

The warming is predicted to cause rising sea levels, larger and more frequent extreme weather events (floods, droughts, and hurricanes), and increased acidity of the oceans. Just how significant these changes will be is difficult to determine, especially if temperatures hit the upper range of the projections or beyond. Most analysts agree that severity of climate disruptions increase at an increasing rate as temperature rises. The economic effects we discuss are for what is believed to be the "most likely" rise in temperature, but the costs could jump sharply if temperatures rise beyond that range.

The difficult job of estimating the economic consequences of climate change requires linking the predictions about temperature change to the impact on the natural world and then relating those environmental changes to effects on human welfare. The human welfare effects arise from changes in agricultural output, the health environment, property values, and in the wildlife that people value. A dollar value is attached to each of these changes, and the total dollar valuation of the welfare loss is expressed as a fraction of GDP. In short, the challenging exercise involves calculating the dollar valuation of the permanent loss in welfare caused by a given increase in temperature. The economic effects of climate change are much more uncertain than the environmental effects, which themselves are quite uncertain (Nordhaus 2018).

An oft-quoted estimate is that a 4.5 °F rise in temperature, a mid-range prediction for warming, is estimated to cause a permanent annual welfare loss equivalent to 1.5% of global GDP. This is a counterfactual calculation that attempts to answer the question, "How much lower would GDP be if we lived in a world that was 4.5 °F warmer?" As temperature gradually increases over several decades to the ultimate 4.5 °F rise, the loss in each decade would be increasing but would be smaller than the estimated 1.5% loss in global GDP. However, the estimated losses rise sharply with any further increases in temperature. Because of the significant uncertainties associated with climate change, the policy response to global warming should be aggressive to provide some *insurance* against the possibility of quite large losses if temperatures rise toward the upper range of estimates or beyond.

Chapter 5 examines the economics of climate change and what new policies are needed to combat global warming in an economically efficient way. Unfortunately, a fully efficient approach to climate policy is not likely to receive sufficient political support in the USA. We also discuss the (second-best) policy changes that may receive enough votes.

One early legislative success is the component of the Inflation Reduction Act 2022 that offers financial incentives for clean energy initiatives in the USA. However, this legislation immediately received criticism from US allies. European countries see the new policy as granting government subsidies to US companies, an action that violates free trade agreements. The controversy highlights the fact that climate policy interacts closely with trade policy. Climate change will also increase the incentive for people to migrate from warmer poor countries to colder rich countries, which will intensify debates over immigration. The policies discussed in Chaps. 4 and 5 are inherently linked and must be coordinated to be effective.

Connections

The economic trends we highlight share the fact that they are fundamentally important to household welfare and are the reason for many of our current ills, both economic and political. Policy makers need to be aware of their close connections. Below, we provide some additional discussion of why a comprehensive approach to policy reforms is needed.

Failed Education Policy Causes Slow Growth, Rising Wage Inequality, Economic Frustration, and the Rise of Populism

The slowdown in average worker productivity growth combined with the widening spread of productivity gains across workers has left most US households with stagnant or declining living standards. Many households struggle to afford housing, education for their children, and medical care, while a relatively small portion of society has no such difficulty. Economic frustration has led to a misplaced search for scapegoats to blame—housing policy, foreign trade and immigration, corporations and the super-rich, unfair labor compensation by firms that are unopposed by labor unions, student loan policy, and an inefficient bloated government that taxes too much and spends wastefully. The economic concerns and political frustration have a common cause—the weakening of average worker productivity growth and the concentration of the productivity gains that do occur among the highly educated.

The country's approach to education is suffering from diminishing returns, a reduced investment in learning, and a misplaced emphasis on traditional college. The way we are educating US workers helps explain both the rise in wage inequality and the slowdown in worker productivity growth rates. Worker productivity growth began to slow as the fraction of young adults that enroll and complete college began to stagnant 40 years ago. The lack of rigor and the lack of quantitative skill formation associated with many college majors have caused some graduates to have disappointing outcomes in the market for high-paying jobs during the twenty-first century. The percent of the work force with a college degree has topped out around 30%, and many of those who do graduate lack the skills needed to be productive workers in today's economy. As a consequence, growth in the nation's human capital and in average worker productivity have slowed dramatically. It also means that only a relatively small fraction of the workforce is receiving high and rising wages, causing wage inequality to worsen.

Economic Frustration Creates Popular Resistance to Needed Reforms of Fiscal, Climate Change, and International Policies

While the lack of wage growth has caused income to remain stagnant for the majority of households, the relative prices of housing, health insurance, and college continue to rise. Increasingly, middle class households view not only housing and health insurance but also college as a risky necessity—a required investment if their children are to have any chance at a decent standard of living. The USA has a culture that exerts strong social pressure to send children to college, a "college-for-all" mentality, with little regard for nonacademic or vocational training. Despite the rising relative cost of tuition and university fees, over half of each age cohort attempts some type of college. Only about one third of each age cohort completes college with a degree in hand. Completion of college is taking longer, which only raises the cost further for those that do graduate.

Discretionary consumption has become increasingly constrained by the lack of real income growth and the rise in the cost of required expenditures in housing, health, and education. Families needing to make the health and education investments that they believe give their children a chance at success in today's economy have become increasingly willing to share the financial burden of these investments with their children. Individually, parents cannot legally leave debt for their children to repay. However, society can pass along unpaid debt through the government. This is one factor creating the popular support for, or at least the lack of opposition to, increased use of public debt. Thus, slow economic growth and rising wage inequality is an important force behind the fiscal crisis.

Economic frustration also reduces the relative importance placed on climate change and poisons attitudes toward globalization because foreigners are a favorite scapegoat of extreme politicians. However, the economic benefits of reducing global warming are becoming more and more clear. One policy that economists recommend to mitigate global warming is to impose a carbon tax. A carbon tax not only discourages the use of energy sources that omit carbon but in addition has the secondary benefit of providing tax revenue to help close the fiscal gap. The negative views of globalization also badly miss the mark. US economic growth benefits from all aspects of globalization. Trade, immigration, and capital mobility are activities we should encourage.

Current Fiscal Policies Crowd Out Private and Public Investment, Reduce Economic Growth, and Are the Primary Source of the Fiscal Crisis

The pay-as-you-go financing of our large retirement programs is not only the primary driver of the fiscal crisis but also undermines national saving and physical capital formation. Beyond the effects of these policies on fiscal solvency, they are slowing economic growth by reducing private investment. The large demands placed on tax revenue to fund old-age programs and debt service also make it difficult to fund government investment. Government investments in R&D and infrastructure have been crowded out of the budget by the rapid expansion of retirement programs. The resulting low level of net investment in private and public capital is another factor pulling down the growth of worker productivity and wages. The full negative impact has not been felt because foreign saving has partially compensated for the decline in national saving. This has created trade imbalances that increase US dependency on countries such as China and is one factor damaging the relations between the world's largest two economies—at a time when the world needs to cooperate to limit global warming. The policy roots of the fiscal crisis are both the cause and consequence of slowing worker productivity growth and indirectly affect all areas of needed policy reform.

Needed Policy Reforms Face Major Political Obstacles

The needed policy reforms to address the negative trends in the USA will be difficult because of vested interests that want to maintain the status quo. The fiscal crisis of this century will primarily be driven by aging and increasingly generous transfers to retirees. The transfers to retirees are promoted by a variety of interest groups representing the elderly and the medical industry. Wage inequality has been rising because of an overly optimistic notion that most of the population benefits, or should benefit, from college and that resources should be disproportionately devoted to the college-prep track in high school—a notion promoted by a variety of interest groups representing universities and the highly educated elite.

The interest groups supporting the current fiscal and education policies are important reasons that real wages have not risen for most households in decades. The resulting economic struggles of the middle class explain the reluctance to seriously address climate change. Most households are concerned about climate change but feel they can't afford the cost of policies needed to deal with it. There is insufficient public push-back against the special interests protecting the status quo energy industry. Similarly, there is weak opposition to the special interests associated with industries that are threatened by foreign competition.

Political Advantage to Comprehensive Reforms

As we have stressed, the fiscal crisis is closely connected to the other two major economic issues of the day: slowing economic growth and rising economic inequality. It is not likely that the fiscal crisis can be permanently resolved without comprehensive policy reforms that deal with these two issues as well. While it is typically the case that policy changes are viewed in isolation, this is not necessarily sensible for both economic and political reasons.

There is a significant political advantage to thinking about reforms broadly. All realistic reforms will involve difficult give-and-take among political parties and interest groups. Thinking simultaneously across several different policy changes expands the possibility for constructive tradeoffs and compromises. In a wonderfully insightful, and even entertaining, summary of Sweden's experience with fiscal consolidation, Jens Henriksson (2007, pp. 18–19) makes this point well.

> Presenting the consolidation measures in one package makes it clear to all interest groups that they are not the only ones being asked to make sacrifices. The idea is to signal that you are not a partisan and that budget deficits is a general problem that everyone should participate in solving.
>
> If one interest group complains, you are in trouble. But if everyone complains you are not.

Summary

The economic challenges of the twenty-first century are closely connected and are to a large extent driven by existing fiscal, education, international, and climate policy of the USA. These connections are summarized in Fig. 1.3. The close connections imply that comprehensive policy reforms should simultaneously address slowing growth, rising inequality, the fiscal crisis, as well as global warming. However, a

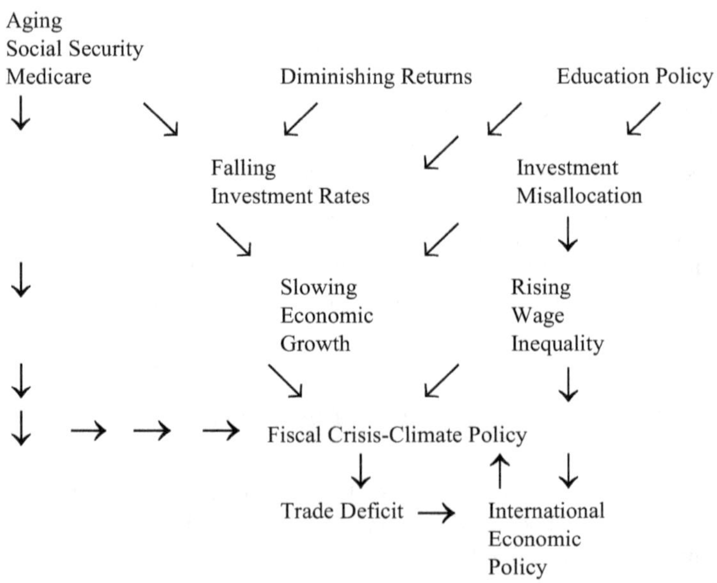

Fig. 1.3 Connections

convincing case must be made for the policy reforms to overcome the vested interests that have supported current policies for so long. We present that case based on evidence from economic research.

References

Alden, E., 2022, "Immigration has Become an Elaborate Bait and Switch," *Foreign Policy*, October 27.

Bilgin, M., Gozgor, G., and Rangazas, P., 2019, "Immigration, Innovation, and Economic Growth," *Singapore Economic Review*, (forthcoming).

Bloom, N., Jones, C., Van Reenen, J., and Webb, M., 2017, "Are Ideas Getting Harder to Find?," *Standford University Working Paper.*

Brynjolfsson, E. and McAfee, A., 2014, *The Second Machine Age: Work, Progress, and Prosperity in a Time of Brilliant Technologies*, New York: WW Norton and Company.

Congressional Budget Office, 2021, *The Long-term Budget Outlook*, March, Washington DC.

Emanuel, K., 2012, *What We Know About Climate Change*, Cambridge, MA.: MIT Press.

Friedman, T. and Mandlebaum, M., 2012, *That Used to be Us*, Picodar: New York.

Goldin, C. and Katz, L., 2008, *The Race between Education and Technology*, Cambridge MA: Harvard University Press.

Gordon, R., 2016, *The Rise and Fall of American Growth: The U.S. Standard of Living since the Civil War*, Princeton University Press: Princeton.

Haskel, J., and Westlake, S., 2017, *Capitalism without Capital: The Rise of the IntangibleEconomy*, Princeton: Princeton University Press.

Hazan, E., Haskel, J., and Westlake, S., 2021, "The Rise of Intangible Capitalism," *ProjectSyndicate*, McKinsey Global Institute, November 12.

Henriksson, J., 2007, "Ten Lessons about Budget Consolidation," *Bruegel Essay and Lecture Series*, Brussels.

Hunt, J., and Gautheir-Loiselle, M., 2010, "How Much Does Immigration Boost Innovation," *American Economic Journal: Macroeconomics*, 2, 31–56.

Jones, C., 2002, "Sources of U.S. Economic Growth in a World of Ideas," *American Economic Review*, 92, 220–239.

Kotlikoff, L., 2015, "America's Fiscal Insolvency and its Generational Consequences," Testimony to the Senate Budget Committee, February 25, 2015.

Lemieux, T., 2010, "What Do We Really Know about Changes in Wage Inequality?," in K. Abraham, M. Harper, J. Spletzer (eds.), *Labor in the New Economy*, University of Chciago Press, 17–59.

Malinovskaya, A., and Wessel, D., 2017, "The Hutchins Center Explains: Public Investment," *Upfront*, Washington: Brooking Institution.

Morkunaite, K., 2019, "A Secular Decline in Capital Productivity in G& Countries," *Intereconomics*, 54, 385–390.

Nordhaus, W., 2018, "Projections and Uncertainties about Climate Change in an Era of Minimal Climate Policies," *American Economic Journal: Economic Policy*, 10(3), 333–360

OECD, 2015, *The Future of Productivity*, Paris: OECD Publishing.

Rachel, L., and Summers, L., 2019, "On Secular Stagnation in an Industrialized World," *Brookings Papers on Economic Activity*, Spring, 1–54

Roubini, N., 2022, *MegaThreats: Ten Dangerous Trends that Imperil Our Future, and How to Survive Them*, New York: Little, Brown, and Company.

Siegel, J., 2023, *Stocks for the Long Run*, New York: McGraw Hill.

Simialek, J., Tankersley, J., and Rennison, J., 2022, "After UK Market Blowout, American Officials Ask: Could It Happen Here? *New York Times*, October 2022.

Tajitsu, N., 2022, “UK Meltdown Raises Spector that Bond Vigilantes are Returning,” *Bloomberg News* September 26.
Valletta, R., 2018, *Education, Skills, and Technical Change: Implications for Future US GDP Growth*, Chicago: University of Chicago Press.
Vijg, J., 2011, *The American Technological Challenge*, New York: Algora Press
Wadhwa, V., 2012, *The Immigrant Exodus*, Philadelphia: Wharton Digital Press.
Wagner, G., and Weitzman, M., 2015, *Climate Shock*, Princeton: Princeton University Press.

Chapter 2
Fiscal Policy

This chapter documents why current US fiscal policies are on an unsustainable path. We discuss the political and economic fundamentals that put the country on this path and the consequences of remaining there going forward. Policy reforms to put government debt on a sustainable path, which may also increase economic growth and reduce income inequality, are then presented.

Before getting into the topic, we need to introduce some fiscal accounting concepts and historical background to place readers on common ground. The change in the outstanding government debt over the course of a year is called the *government budget deficit*. When the deficit is positive, it means that government spending exceeds tax revenue, and new bonds are sold to make up for the difference. If the deficit is negative, it means that tax revenue exceeds government spending, and the government is said to run a *surplus*. With a positive surplus, the excess tax revenue is used to buy back or pay off government debt, so the amount of outstanding debt falls.

The deficit has been persistently positive for four decades (with the exception of a brief 4-year period at the end of the twentieth century). Annual deficits must be quite large for government debt to not only rise but to rise faster than a country's output of goods and services (GDP). In this case, the ratio of government debt to GDP trends upward, as it has in the USA for over 40 years. A continual rise in the government debt-to-GDP ratio is *unsustainable* because at some point the government will be unable to find lenders to buy the debt it needs to issue.

When lenders become at all nervous that the government will be unable to issue sufficient new debt to meet its obligations to repay existing debt, then lenders sell off their current debt holdings, causing bond prices to collapse and interest rates to soar. We saw a glimpse of this recently when the bond market in the UK became concerned about its government's large deficit policy proposal. It is impossible to predict exactly when the bond market loses confidence but when it happens a severe economic downturn is possible as asset values fall, private borrowing costs increase, and the economy's demand for goods declines.

© The Author(s), under exclusive license to Springer Nature Switzerland AG 2023
A. Mourmouras, P. Rangazas, *US Economic Policy in the 21st Century*,
Professional Practice in Governance and Public Organizations,
https://doi.org/10.1007/978-3-031-36437-2_2

The Unsustainable US Fiscal Path

An important and undervalued institution of the US government is the Congressional Budget Office (CBO). The job of the CBO is to assess current and proposed federal fiscal policies in terms of their budgetary feasibility and likely economic consequences. The CBO was created in 1974 and its first director, Alice Rivlin, created a culture of fiercely objective and nonpartisan analysis that has largely been maintained to this day.

Each year, the CBO publishes a report, *The Long-Term Budget Outlook*, forecasting the path of the government debt-to-GDP ratio over the next 30 years assuming current policies remain in place over the period. The CBO measures what is called *government debt held by the public*, i.e., debt held outside of the federal government. This includes debt held by the US central bank but not debt held in the Social Security and Medicare trust funds, which are included in a larger debt measure called *gross government debt.*

Government debt in the trust funds is accumulated when payroll tax revenue (earmarked for Social Security and Medicare) exceeds current benefit payouts and is transferred to the general accounts of the federal government in exchange for government bonds. The government bonds are eventually repaid to finance future benefits from general income tax revenue. The portion of the retirement programs that are financed in this way are essentially "fully funded" because the payroll tax is saved for the retiree via the purchase of government debt. The effects of fully funding retirement programs are different, and less harmful to the economy as a whole, than the primary pay-as-you-go (PAYG) funding mechanism.[1] This is the main reason that the distinction between debt held by the public and gross debt should be made.

The CBO's debt ratio projections require assumptions about future growth rates of GDP and the future interest rates paid on government debt. Higher GDP growth lowers the numerator of the debt ratio, by indirectly increasing tax revenue collected, and raises the denominator of the ratio directly. Interest rates are important because with high and rising government debt, interest payments on the debt are becoming a larger component of government spending. The government issues debt with securities of various maturities but a key interest rate for financial markets and for assessing the government's interest expense is the rate associated with the 10-year Treasury note.

The March 2021 *Outlook* projected the debt ratio out to 2051 based on laws enacted by that January. The projections included the pandemic stimulus and relief spending in 2020 but missed the $1.9 trillion American Rescue Plan passed in March 2021 and the even larger proposed physical and human infrastructure legislation. Due to the recovery from the sharp pandemic recession, the CBO assumed unusually high economic growth rates for the next couple of years before growth returns to its

[1] For an exposition of why national saving falls with PAYG social security, in contrast to a *fully funded* pension program, see Appendix 1 of this Chapter and Ivanyna et al. (2021, section 5.3).

recent historical average. It assumed interest rates on the 10-year note will remain low until 2026. For example, their assumption for 2021 is 1.1%, for 2022 is 1.3%, and for 2023 is 1.5%. However, interest rates have turned out to rise much faster than expected. By the middle of 2021, they already have exceeded 1.5% and were above 3.5% by the end of 2022 (with a rapid rise in real or inflation-adjusted rates as well). Given the faster than expected rise in interest rates, it seems likely that the projections will underestimate the actual rise in debt. Nevertheless, even when assuming low interest rates, the CBO predicts the debt ratio will essentially double over the next 30 years, reaching about 200% in 2051.

Until recently, 2016 to be precise, the CBO projected out 75 years rather than just 30 years. A non-profit organization called the Committee for a Responsible Federal Budget picked up the mantle and attempted to replicate the CBO's 75-year projection methodology in late 2018. They missed the dramatic events that have made the fiscal outlook worse, so their 2050 projection was below 200%. However, by 2093 their (underestimated) projection was frightening enough, a debt ratio of almost 400%.

Very few believe that the rise in the debt ratios of this magnitude are sustainable, so why hasn't the financial market reacted? Investors around the world continue to add US government debt to their portfolios, with relatively low interest rate compensation, because they believe the USA will successfully reform to a sustainable policy stance in the future. However, it is becoming increasingly difficult for the USA to change its fiscal course. There are ways to assess just how far the policy stance must deviate from the current one to make it sustainable as we discuss below.

The Government Intertemporal Budget Constraint

One approach to quantifying the needed fiscal reforms assumes that the government is either unwillingly or unable to do forever what it is currently doing, that is, use new debt to pay off the principal and interest on old debt—the government equivalent of a "Ponzi Game." In technical terms, the No Ponzi Game (NPG) assumption means that fiscal policy is limited by the Government Intertemporal Budget Constraint (GIBC), which says that the sum of current outstanding debt plus the present value of current and future government spending must equal the present value of current and future taxes.

Satisfying the GIBC implies that future surpluses must be run to pay off existing debt obligations. Instead of perpetually issuing new debt to pay off old debt, at some point taxes must be raised in excess of *non-debt related* government spending, what is called the *primary surplus*, to finance debt repayment. The most compact way to state the GIBC is the *present value of future primary surpluses must equal the current value of outstanding debt.*

The USA frequently ran primary surpluses in the middle of the twentieth century, helping to shrink the debt-to-GDP ratio after WWII for more than 30 years (Cochrane 2021, Ch.5). Since then, primary deficits have become the norm, causing a dramatic violation of the GIBC. In 2015, before the fiscal picture worsened significantly, the prominent economist Laurence Kotlikoff presented the fiscal situation to the US senate (Kotlikoff 2015). Instead of future primary surpluses, our current fiscal policies project out to create future primary deficits, indicating a severe shortage of future tax revenue. The revenue shortfalls imply unfunded government liabilities written into our policies, a type of *implicit debt*. The implicit debt of the USA at that time was 16 times larger than the explicit outstanding debt. The sum of the explicit and implicit debt created a *fiscal gap* of $210 trillion that would have to be closed for the government to satisfy the GIBC.

Assuming the steps toward fiscal responsibility occurred promptly in 2015, Kotlikoff reported that the deviations from our current policies needed to close the fiscal gap were dramatic. Suppose we did it exclusively by raising more tax revenue. This required an immediate and permanent increase in federal tax revenue of 60%. Suppose instead we did it exclusively by cutting federal spending. This required an immediate and permanent cut in federal spending of 40%. Delays in taking some combination of these actions, "kicking the can farther down the road," only raised the magnitude of the necessary changes and placed greater burdens on young and future generations.

Sustainable Fiscal Policies

Auerbach (1994) and Auerbach et al. (2018) define the fiscal gap differently. Instead of defining the gap associated with satisfying the GIBC or the NPG condition, they define the gap as what is needed to maintain the debt-to-GDP ratio at some targeted value. The two definitions can be quite different *if* the economy is growing sufficiently fast to allow new debt to be used to pay off old debt *and interest* without violating the targeted debt ratio. Relatively fast growth in GDP allows the government to issue new debt that repays old debt and interest without a rise in the debt-to-GDP *ratio*.

In producing its 30-year debt projections, the CBO assumes that the growth rate of GDP exceeds interest rates, which allows the government to violate the NPG condition. Using CBO estimates, Gale (2019) conducts a study of the necessary fiscal changes needed to target and sustain a debt ratio of 60% of GDP by 2050. While the fiscal reforms are not as large as those needed to satisfy the GIBC, they are still dramatic. If implemented in 2025, there would have to be a permanent increase in federal taxes of 28% or a permanent cut in non-interest federal spending of 24%. The Committee for a Responsible Federal Budget (2022a) carried out a similar exercise. It believes a 50% debt ratio would be ideal but, based on political constraints, offers a plan to stabilize the debt ratio at around its current value of 100%.

It is important to note that sustainability requires fiscal consolidation (tax increases-spending cuts) even when interest rates are low and below GDP rates (more on this in our discussion of interest rates later in the chapter). Many mistakenly believe that interest rates below growth rates imply a country has a "free-lunch," allowing the government to avoid the need for consolidation altogether. The large policy reforms needed to reach even high sustainable debt targets, despite low interest rates assumptions, suggests that out current fiscal stance is far from sustainable.

Economic Effects of Sustainable Intergenerational Redistribution

The danger of a financial market reaction leading to a severe recession and the unfairness of the fiscal burden we are imposing on young and future generations are only two of the costs of our fiscal stance. Sustainable fiscal policies, *even those that satisfy the GIBC*, can have negative economic consequences for future generations.

For example, the expansion of PAYG retirement and health insurance programs for the elderly since the second half of the twentieth century is one of the factors explaining the 10 percentage point decline in net national saving (Kotlikoff (2015) and Rachel and Summers 2019). As a result, net domestic investment has also declined, although not as steeply because of the influx of foreign funding (see Fig. 1.2 in Chap. 1). The decline in net investment has reduced worker productivity growth, making wages lower for workers today and into the future. Even if we make entitlement programs sustainable going forward, the negative effect on future wages will persist.

The Government Investment Gap

We have discussed three ways that our fiscal policy is placing burdens on young and future generations: (i) short-run disruptions of a likely financial crisis, (ii) the austerity associated with the subsequent fiscal reforms, and (iii) the crowding out of private capital formation that slows wage growth. An additional concern is the composition of government spending has been biased toward consumption for decades.

Much of the fiscal gap is due to unfunded programs that support consumption of the elderly. The rise in government funding for the consumption of retired households and the servicing of outstanding debt has been associated with a decline of government *investment* in productive public goods such as roads, bridges, ports, and utilities. Public capital not only directly raises productivity but also complements private capital in production, helping to maintain the return to private investment.[2]

Government infrastructure investment in the USA measured about 3.5% of GDP in 1970. Today, it is about 2.5% and net infrastructure investment is currently only

[2] See Ivanyna et al. (2021, sections 2.6–2.7, 4.6 and 5.2.2).

0.5%. Net *federal* investment has dipped below zero after being almost 1% in the 1980s. As a result of this decline, the public infrastructure of the USA has depreciated to an embarrassing state for such a rich country, contributing to our growth slowdown.[3] The level of US infrastructure investment is so obviously deficient that, despite unprecedented political division, the Infrastructure and Jobs Act was passed in 2021. This Act and some aspects of the more recent Inflation Reduction Act of 2022 reflect encouraging policy movements in the direction of the recommendations found in this book.

Another important public investment is the financing of basic research. Basic research yields general results in science and mathematics. The findings of basic research have profitable spinoffs through the creation of a variety of new private sector goods. The risk and costs of this kind of research are too high for individual firms and venture capitalists to finance because of the difficulty in capturing a share of all the potential spinoff benefits.[4]

The fraction of federal funding for the basic research, which lays the foundation for technological progress, was cut over the last quarter of the twentieth century. In the mid-1960s, federal funding for research and development was 2% of GDP. Today it has dipped to well below 1%.[5] In addition to budget pressures that are crowding out funding for public investment, there is the concern that individual governments now face reduced incentives to invest in basic research because of the increased ease of international spillovers of knowledge. If each country attempts to free ride off the basic research of other countries, technological progress across the globe will fall.

Weak government investment is one of the reasons for the decline in worker productivity growth. It also means that the burdens of the fiscal gap will be harder for future generations to bear because of diminished real wage growth, which has also been weakened by declining national saving due to PAYG retirement programs and expanding government debt. For the sake of future generations, the government needs to not only close the fiscal gap but also restore its investment in the future. In the middle of the twentieth century, the US government was investing 5.5% of GDP in infrastructure and basic research. Today that has fallen to 3.2%. To remove the 2 percentage point investment gap between the period of strong growth in the mid-twentieth century and today will require additional funding in the form of spending cuts and tax increases beyond what is necessary to close the fiscal gap under current policy.

---

[3] See Friedman and Mandlebaum (2012), Malinovskaya and Wessel (2017), and Gale (2019).

[4] For examples of the crucial role played by basic research in private product development and economic growth, see Ivanyna et al. (2021, section 4.6) and Gruber and Johnson (2019, Chapter 5).

[5] Gruber and Johnson (2019, Chapters 3 and 4) discuss reasons for the decline and why private research and development cannot substitute for the missing government support.

Money Financing and the COVID-19 Recession

The US recession caused by COVID-19 would have been much worse if not for a massive policy response on the part of the federal government and the central bank (the "Fed," short for the Federal Reserve). In quick fashion, the federal government passed the CARES Act to bolster incomes of the many households and small businesses. The combined effect of the new legislation, the loss of tax revenue due to the shrinking tax base, and the automatic increases in spending that occur when incomes fall (such are Medicaid and Food Stamps) caused 2.5 trillion dollars in federal government debt to be issued from the beginning of March 2020 to the beginning of June 2020. By the end of 2020, the federal deficit exceeded $3 trillion. The pre-COVID projection for 2020 was a trillion-dollar deficit. After the passage of the American Rescue Plan in March 2021, the federal deficit was projected to reach $3.4 trillion in 2021.

The Fed's actions were even more dramatic. It ramped up its usual practice of increasing private bank reserves to lower the Federal Funds interest rate in the overnight credit market used by bankers. It also took the bigger steps of lowering the discount rate charged to private banks when they borrow from the central bank and reducing private bank capital requirements to encourage the private banks to lend more. Deviating from business as usual, the Fed became very active as the "lender of last resort" in all sorts of credit markets. In the government bond market, the Fed purchased 1.6 trillion dollars of government debt, out of the 2.5 trillion issued to finance the deficit as of mid-year 2020. Thus, well over half of the rise in the government deficit was financed by "printing money" rather than by borrowing from the private sector and foreign sources. This is because when the Fed purchases newly issued debt, it gives the government cash, not previously in circulation, to spend on their programs. In addition, the Fed set up special facilities allowing them to directly lend to virtually everyone: corporations, mid-size businesses, nonprofits, state and local governments, as well as international central banks.

The large spending stimulus provided by fiscal and monetary policy was widely supported by politicians, economists, and the general public. The policy response was necessary to help minimize the sharp drop in economic activity beginning in March 2020. There was much uncertainty over the exact path of the virus, and it was appropriate that central authorities did what they could to limit the economic damage. However, this does not eliminate the *long-run* negative consequences associated with the massive increases in government debt financed by central bank purchases. Economies are seeing these consequences now in unusually high inflation rates.[6] Inflation is the reason that monetary policy is not a long-run solution to a fiscal crisis.

---

[6]To be sure supply-side shocks have also contributed to the rise in inflation. Supply-side shocks have taken a variety of forms due to the pandemic—disruptions in modes of domestic production, reductions in labor supply, and breaking of international supply chains. The Russian-Ukraine war has added to these shocks through a reduction in food and energy supplies. However, di Giovanni

Long-Run Economic Effects

The large stimulus needed to keep economies afloat during the pandemic has worsened an already precarious long-run fiscal position in many countries. Before the pandemic, the US debt-to-GDP ratio was projected to rise from a value of approximately 80% in 2020 to 100% by 2030. Due to the appearance of COVID-19, the projection for 2030 has jumped to well beyond 100% (to historical highs exceeding even the WWII period).

As we have previously mentioned, the USA has been fortunate to service its public debt in recent decades at very low interest rates. Despite its anemic national saving rate, the USA has expanded its debt at low interest rates because foreign lending has also expanded. Currently foreigners hold about 40% of outstanding US debt. However, there are reasons to believe that the USA will finally be reaching the limit of its cheap funding. Foreigners have only financed 20% of newly issued government debt over the last decade, causing the fraction of total government debt held by foreigners to dip from 50% to the current value of 40%. The contribution from our previously large lenders, China and Japan, has barely increased over this period. The largest international lenders to the USA over the decade have been the UK (despite its own deficit issues) and Ireland.

The increasingly poisoned relations with China suggest there will now be less lending to the USA and the large European stimulus response to the pandemic, and more recently due to the Russian-Ukrainian war, it has reduced Europe's ability to lend abroad. Japan has been moving against the current global trend where central banks are raising interest rates by cutting back on government bond purchases. They have continued to issue new currency (the yen), which includes exchanging yen for dollars and then using the dollars to purchase US government bonds. However, the yen is experiencing rapid depreciation, and Japan is showing signs of reversing its easy money-low interest rate policy. This would mean less Japanese lending to the USA.

The USA has been able to absorb the sharp increase in debt during 2020 in part because of a dramatic rise in precautionary saving by its own households and firms (along with plenty of help from the Fed). However, as the pandemic subsides and the recovery strengthens, the saving rate is declining back to its low long-run level. It should also be remembered that the largest source of the long-run fiscal crisis comes from the unfunded social programs. The drop in payroll tax revenue because of the pandemic in the USA has moved up the projected date when entitlement program trust funds will be exhausted, to as early as 2031 for Social Security and 2028 for Medicare. At these dates, benefits would have to be significantly cut unless payroll tax rates are raised. Where will the USA find lenders willing to buy all the newly issued government debt?

---

et al. (2022) estimates that in the USA about 1/3 of the inflation emanates from the supply side while 2/3 is due to an expansion in nominal spending.

This scenario means the Fed and other central banks will be pressured to continue their roles as the lenders to the government. Even after economies recover, the shortages of funds will put pressure on central banks to purchase government debt and essentially money-finance deficits as we move into the middle of this century. These pressures are supported by the unusual inflation record of the last few decades before the pandemic. Large money supply increases during times of normal economic activity have historically led to higher inflation. However, during the early twenty-first century, and especially since the Great Recession of 2008, the close link between money growth and inflation has been broken. The break between money growth and inflation has left the incorrect impression that money financing of persistent government deficits is a sensible approach.[7]

From late 2008 to late 2016, annual money growth averaged in the neighborhood of 10%, yet inflation was 2–3%. Inflation stayed low because the velocity of money, the rate at which each dollar is spent, was falling or, put another way, the willingness to hold money in the form of reserves was rising. This was because the opportunity cost of holding money rather than interest-bearing assets was falling. The decline in the cost of holding money was due to a combination of the long downward trend in market real interest rates, which began after 1980, and the new Fed policy of paying interest on reserves, which began in 2008. Since 2008, the difference between bonds, loans, and money has blurred and the opportunity cost of holding money has become small. This means the Fed can swap reserves for (short-term) bonds more easily because banks and individuals view the two as roughly equivalent. The massive purchases of government bonds with new reserves during 2020 and 2021 caused no significant changes in market prices or interest rates because the reserves were simply absorbed and willing held.[8] The new role of the Fed, as seen by some, was to guarantee sufficient demand for debt during the pandemic and beyond.

However, during 2022, the unusually large increases in the money supply during the pandemic have contributed to a spike in inflation rates not seen for 40 years. The Fed was late to respond to the rise in prices and is now playing catch-up by raising short-term interest rates, allowing government debt to mature off its balance sheets, and resisting the purchases of newly issued government debt. Nominal and real interest rates on short-term and long-term government debt have risen rapidly. The rise in real interest rates means that bonds will once again become distinctly different from reserves. It also means that more future debt will have to be issued to service the debt sold with higher interest rate promises. In this setting, even if the Fed were to buy the additional debt that is issued, the reserves will no longer be willingly held

[7] Proponents of Modern Monetary Theory (MMT) have pushed the idea of using money creation as a way of financing government deficits. The rise of inflation during the last 2 years casts serious doubt on this policy prescription. One should be suspicious of MMT in general. As pointed out by Mankiw (2020, p. 141), "MMT was developed in a small corner of academia and became famous only when some high-profile politicians—particularly Senator Bernie Sanders and Representative Alexandria Ocasio-Cortez—drew attention to it because its tenets conformed to their policy views."

[8] For more discussion on the effects of monetary policy and the relationship between reserves and bonds, see Cochrane (2021, Chapters 12–14) and Saving (2019).

and instead will be spent, causing inflation to jump further. The Fed simply cannot finance persistent government budget deficits. It is having enough trouble controlling inflation, which requires that they sell back, not purchase, government debt.

New Generational Tensions

The generational conflict associated with the fiscal crisis has worsened because of the pandemic. Reduced economic activity, due to voluntary and involuntary attempts to increase social distancing and suppress the virus, disproportionately benefits older retired households and disproportionately hurts younger working households and students. The extra debt associated with the government stimulus will also disproportionately burden younger generations as government programs are cut and taxes are increased in the future to service the new debt and prevent additional borrowing.

These generational considerations only increased the pressure on central bankers to continue buying government debt and increase the money supply even after the virus dissipated and economies began to recover. As mentioned, continued money growth after the economy started growing has increased inflation rates. Late in 2021 and throughout 2022, we have seen US inflation rates spike to their highest values since the infamous inflation of the 1970s and early 1980s. Nominal interest rates on debt issued previous to and during the pandemic did not anticipate this large increase in inflation. This means older households have been hurt by inflation because they are locked into the low-interest government bonds purchased in the past. In the short run, the accommodating monetary stance helps the government repay debt because tax revenue increases as inflation pushes nominal incomes higher, while the interest expenses on bonds issued before the rise in inflationary expectations stay fixed. The more inflation is used to repay debt, the fewer tax rate increases, or spending cuts will be needed, which helps younger generations that have not yet built up their retirement savings and are not currently holding much of the low-interest government debt.

The ability to use inflation as a way of reducing debt burdens is partly a function of the types of government securities outstanding. Money growth and inflation is most effective as a government revenue source when the outstanding debt is composed of securities with longer maturity because the asset holders are locked into low-interest rates for a longer period before the government has to refinance with newly issued debt (at higher interest rates that reflect the rise in inflationary expectations). The average maturity of US debt is currently about 5 years, so there is some scope for using inflation as a substitute for tax rate increases or spending cuts to service debt obligations.

The short-run advantage of money financing dissipates as nominal interest rates rise on newly issued government debt. In addition, inflation does nothing to reduce the burden of the government's unfunded liabilities under its entitlement programs. The benefits under Social Security, and effectively under Medicare insurance as well, are indexed to the rate of inflation. Thus, as nominal tax revenue rises with inflation, so will the nominal payments under the large transfers programs.

Using monetary policy and inflation to finance government debt is common in middle-income countries where central banks are more directly tied to the government. Central banks in advanced economies have become more independent from their governments over the twentieth century and have not typically been willing to use money creation to finance government budget deficits. Central bank behavior during the pandemic has shifted dramatically, and concerns over generational fairness provide another reason to attempt money financing of government deficits. However, the spike in inflation rates have become public enemy number one to the American public and will limit the Federal Reserve's willingness to use money creation to finance budget deficits going forward. By mid-2022, the Fed began allowing their holdings of government debt to mature without replacing them with new debt purchases. Money financing of large portions of our budget deficits is over (we hope).

There are alternatives to inflation that the government could use to shift the burden of its public debt to older households. A sensible alternative is to institute a federal consumption tax as part of the fiscal reform. While retired households can avoid wages taxation from payroll and income taxes, this is not true of a consumption tax.

A more dramatic alternative, which was threatened during the Trump administration, is to simply default on interest and principal repayments to public debt holders. Default is a risky approach because if the market senses this, as even a possibility, it could force the government's hand by selling off government bonds and driving interest rates up to the point that default is the government's only practical alternative. If default occurs, how will the government find the ever-greater quantity of loanable funds needed to finance government programs throughout the century? The only viable way to have older generations contribute to the needed fiscal reforms is to include a consumption tax component.

Public Health Policy

We have focused on the fiscal and monetary response to the pandemic. The response was an attempt to prevent an economic collapse caused by voluntary and mandated lockdowns that severely disrupted economic activity. One could also consider an analysis of the *public health* response designed to check the spread of the virus, which would include lockdowns as a possible policy tool. Identifying the economic consequences of different public health responses is an important and, until recently, largely unexplored area of research.

The significant economic and health impact of COVID has motivated an assessment of the best health policy mix to stop the spread of a contagious disease while weighing the economic cost of the possible government interventions and recommendations. Economists have adapted models of disease spread from the epidemiology literature to include economic components that account for possible output effects and behavioral changes caused by health policy interventions.

The research is too preliminary to provide definitive policy advice, but it is building toward that end. One example is a study by Alvarez et al. (2020). Their study designs a way to include both the economic value of life lost from infection and the economic value of output lost from lockdowns. They calculate the optimal intensity and duration of lockdowns that minimize the total economic loss. The calculations are based on parameter settings and initial conditions that capture important factors such as the percent of the population initially infected, the effectiveness of lockdowns at preventing disease spread, the fatality rate for those catching the virus, available hospital capacity, and the presence of vaccines and cures.

Another example is Carnehl et al. (2022) where the focus is on voluntary individual choices about costly social distancing, choices that will vary with the policy interventions in ways that have not been modeled in past work. An interesting feature of their model is that the effectiveness of policy interventions, such as mask mandates, can be compromised by individuals becoming more willing to take the risk of engaging in normal social interaction.

Other related research is of a more immediate practical nature. The Center for Disease Control (CDC 2022) has conducted a self-study with the aim of learning from mistakes it made in coordinating scientific effort, informing the public about the nature of the virus, and making policy recommendations. One of the conclusions is that the CDC should shift its focus to coordinating *outside* research efforts, rather than conducting its own in-house research, and then clearly communicating the findings and related recommendations to the public.

The Crucial Role of Interest Rates

The USA has not seriously contemplated fiscal reforms because it has been able to borrow at unusually low real interest rates. The low rates make it easier to service debt obligations and to use money financing without igniting inflation. To determine whether interest rates will remain at or near current levels, we need to know why they fell to historical lows to begin with.

Why Are Interest Rates Low?

Increasingly, interest rates are determined by global, and not only national, forces. The average global real interest rate on 10-year government debt has trended downward over the last 40 years from 6.3% in 1983 to approximately zero in 2012, and during the pandemic, real interest rates have become negative. An IMF study by Furceri and Pescatori (2014) identifies the following factors that led to the decline. First, strong growth in emerging (middle-income) countries raised income levels and caused an increase in their savings rates, shifting the global supply of funds up over time. Second, for at least a decade after the Great Recession, the stock market was viewed as becoming riskier. The experience of the 2007 financial crisis caused risk-averse savers to change their portfolio mix in favor of safe US government bonds, causing the risk-free rate to fall further than returns to riskier equity assets. Third, there has been a decline in investment rates in middle-income and advanced economies that have shifted the global demand for funds down. The two forces increasing the supply of funds and the one force reducing the demand for funds caused an excess supply of funds, a savings "glut," that lowered the equilibrium interest rates in international capital markets. Since the Great Recession, the decline in government bond rates reflects both shifts in overall saving and investment as well as a change in the composition of saving toward safer and more liquid government debt.

A study by Rachel and Summers (2019) documents the decline in interest rates as a long-term trend that precedes the Great Recession, stretching back to the 1980s. They argue that the decline is predominately due to changes in overall saving and investment (rather than the composition of saving). In fact, they suggest that forces within the *private* sector of advanced economies would have led to an even greater decline in real interest rates than what was observed. The observed real interest rates were kept higher because of the negative effect of government deficits and PAYG retirement programs on national savings and the supply of funds. Without the fiscal forces, real interest rates would have fallen by another 3 percentage points, pushing them even farther into the negative range.

Rachel and Summers do not provide direct empirical evidence on the precise private forces that caused saving to increase and investment to fall, for given interest rates (i.e. "shifts in saving and investment curves"). However, they developed models to judge what might be reasonable candidates. The analysis points to reduced growth rates of technical progress and increased aging with longer retirements, two forces that could both raise saving and reduce investment.

It is important to note that, unlike many others, they do *not* suggest that China's emergence in the global economy had much of an effect. Rachel and Summers argue that advanced countries with large gaps between domestic investments and national saving, such as the USA, could have been funded by other countries in the advanced world, such as Germany and Japan, in the absence of funding from China. Of course, the absence of China's saving would presumably imply a decrease in international loanable funds available to middle- and low-income countries. China, while perhaps not critical to funding the USA alone, nevertheless played a role in keeping global interest rates low.

Cochrane (2021, Chapter 7) also emphasizes private forces within advanced economies as the reason for the real interest rate decline. He focuses on decreases in investment demand rather than increases in private savings. He sees trend features that have pulled down the return to private capital such as greater government regulation, inadequate government infrastructure investment, and a decreasing effective labor supply (partly due to aging as mentioned above).

In summary, the decline in real interests is undeniably a long-term trend. The most important fundamentals causing interest rates to be unusually low cannot primarily be recent events such large-scale government bond purchases by central banks, a flight to safety after the Great Recession, or China's greater presence in the world economy. Research tells us that the most important fundamentals come from within the private sector of advanced economies. The best candidates are reduced technical progress, slowing growth in the effective labor supply (the skill-adjusted workforce), and inadequate infrastructure investment, all three of which lowered the return to private physical capital and investment demand and an expansion in longevity and retirement that expanded private saving.

Will Interest Rates Remain Low?

If interest rates are to remain low, the private sector fundamentals keeping them low must remain in place. However, two of the fundamentals seem likely to reverse themselves and push interest rates back up.

First, there has been a recent political movement to raise government infrastructure, and perhaps more basic research funding will follow. An increase in public capital increases an important input to production that is complementary to private capital. In addition, technical progress may pick up as the stock of basic knowledge increases if there is increased government support for research. Expanding government investment generally makes so much sense at this time and benefits such a wide segment of the population that politicians may not be able to say no. In the politically divided USA, there was bipartisan support for significant increases in physical infrastructure investment, as seen in the passing of the Infrastructure Investment and Jobs Act of 2021. Second, as aging and longevity continues to unfold over the century, there be will larger fractions of the world population that are dis-saving their accumulated assets during retirement, thereby lowering private saving.

Even absent a reversal of private forces holding interest rates down, one could nevertheless expect a sustained rise in rates. As documented above, public debt and PAYG financed retirement programs are projected to expand rapidly over the century. The resulting shortage of funds and the rise in real rates caused by these policies could exceed the 3 percentage increase identified by Rachel and Summers (2019) over the last 40 years. Thus, there are good reasons to expect a rise in interest rates emanating from forces in both the private and public sectors.

If Interest Rates Do Remain Low, Does the Fiscal Crisis Disappear?

The chapter *Appendix 2* shows that if, despite the forces we have identified, interest rates do remain below the growth in GDP, it is then possible for the government to successfully run a Ponzi game (violating the GIBC) while at the same time maintaining a sustainable debt-to-GDP ratio. New debt can be issued in sufficient quantities to repay old debt and interest without causing a rise in the debt-to-GDP ratio because the growth rate of debt will be smaller than the growth rate of GDP. In fact, a constant debt-to-GDP ratio could be maintained in this situation while running a primary deficit. Some of the growth in new debt could be used to cover a shortfall of taxes needed to match non-debt-related government spending.

However, the analysis in *Appendix 2* also shows that even with low interest rates (i.e., below the growth rate of GDP), sustainability requires *some* policy discipline about the size of the primary deficit. Low interest rates do not allow the government to run *any* primary deficit that is convenient. This is why Gale (2019) had to work to find the right policy reforms needed to match a debt ratio target of 60%. So far not much has been done in the way of significant reforms. Policies have only become more pro-debt, and the debt-to-GDP ratio is rising over time *despite* a period of unusually low interest rates.

If Interest Rates Do Remain Low, What Should the Government Do to Exploit the Opportunity?

In economic models that assume perfect certainty, all assets that are willingly held must pay the same return. The rate of return to physical capital and the interest rate on government debt must be equal. In this setting, if the common rate of return on assets is lower than the growth rate of the economy, the government can unambiguously make all generations, currently alive and in the future, better off by redistributing income from young household to old household in every period.

For example, PAYG social security would be an especially good idea despite the fact that it crowds out private capital formation. The implicit return households receive from the net lifetime effect of the government transfer scheme (due to the growth rate of wage as base for the payroll tax) beats the return households could get from private assets. In addition, the reduction in private capital is actually a good thing because the positive welfare effect of driving up the marginal product of capital and the rate of return on assets beats the negative welfare effect of lowering the marginal product of labor and wages.[9] In this low-return scenario, the pre-policy

[9] Higher physical capital intensity lowers the marginal product of capital and rates of return while raising the marginal product of labor and wages. Which of these effects dominates in determining the change in household welfare depends on the initial degree of physical capital intensity. For an

economy has "too much" physical capital and is called *dynamically inefficient* because a Ponzi-like government intervention makes every generation better off. This justification for PAYG social security, and other perpetual "debt-rollover" policies, was established in a classical paper by Peter Diamond (1965).

There are extensions of the simple overlapping-generations model used by Diamond where unpredictable productivity shocks make output and the return to physical capital uncertain. In this setting, there are *two* average rates of return: a high average return on risky private capital and a low interest rate on safe government debt (as in actual economies). A calibration of such a model that seeks to fit recent observations would make the average rate of return to capital higher than the economy's average growth rate which, in turn, is higher than the risk-free interest rate. Under these assumptions, it is tempting to try government Ponzi schemes because of the low interest rate on safe government debt. The problem is that in the calibration just described there is not "too much" physical capital, as indicated by an average rate of return above the economy's growth rate. Less private capital now lowers welfare because the effect of lower wages dominates the effect of higher rates of return. Ponzi schemes remain potentially attractive but now they bring the costs of reducing high-return physical capital. The crowding out of private capital can bite future generations enough to lower their lifetime welfare. The ambiguous welfare implications of this scenario are presented clearly by Olivier Blanchard (2019).[10]

To resolve the ambiguity, Blanchard simulates numerically constructed Ponzi schemes in the extended overlapping-generations model and finds that frequently, but by no means always, a policy intervention makes all generations better off. Brumm et al. (2021) generalize Blanchard's model in various ways and do a more extensive simulation analysis of different Ponzi policies. They find that in the most realistic calibrations, the welfare of future generations consistently fall due to the quantitatively dominant negative effect associated with a lower stock of private capital.

In summary, there is little justification for increasing PAYG social security or rolling over greater quantities of public debt to finance more government transfers and consumption when safe interest rates are unusually low. The case is better for increasing government investment financed by borrowing because greater public capital would raise wages, the return to private capital on average, and perhaps even the private capital stock. However, even here the welfare case is sketchy because it is ambiguous when the positive effect of more public capital will also raise private capital. If private capital falls due to the debt used to finance public investments, an empirical analysis is needed to determine if the incomes of future generations will be higher. There is currently a good case for more government investment because

exposition of the connection between physical capital intensity, rates of return, and wages, see Ivanyna (2021, Chapter 4). For the connection to household welfare, see Blanchard (2019).

[10] Another drawback of trying government Ponzi schemes in this setting is that they could collapse. When crowding out of private capital becomes significant, it becomes difficult, and even impossible, to collect enough taxes from workers to pay any given promised benefit to retirees. See Rangazas and Russell (2005).

public capital per capita has deteriorated and the marginal return is relatively high. However, the financing should be conducted in a way that minimizes the chance of reducing the private capital stock. Even when used to fund public investment, government debt is not the best financing approach for raising the welfare of future generations.

Waiting for Fiscal Reforms

Fiscal policy reforms are necessary because the current fiscal path will eventually lead to large shortages of government funding, resulting in a major financial crisis across the developed world. There is a fair degree of consensus among economists that the reforms suggested, for example, by Gale (2019) are at least reasonable starting points for the policy discussion. What is much less clear is whether the reforms will be passed in a timely way, especially given the ineffectiveness of political systems in advanced countries and especially in the USA.

Allan Drazen (2000, p. 403), an expert on the political economy of macroeconomics, succinctly summarizes the issue this way:

> in situations in which economic arguments clearly favor reform, one must look to political constraints to understand why reforms are not enacted or sustained, or are only enacted after long delay.

Current political systems are characterized by corruption, disproportionate influence of interest groups on policy, polarization of political philosophy among policy makers, and a bias to subsidize consumption rather than investment—all factors that many feel have become larger problems over time and that have led to the fiscal crisis to begin with. How confident can we be that the same politics will generate timely and effective reforms?

One theory is that an economic crisis is needed to generate compromise among conflicting interests that ends in meaningful reform (Drazen 2000, Chapter 10). This is a pessimistic view because one would hope that policy changes would help *avert* crises well before they happen. However, the view that crisis leads to reform may actually be *too optimistic* in practice. Consider the quote from the long-time US politician, Leon Panetta, found in Wessel (2012, p. 162).

> I used to tell students that we are either governed by leadership or crisis. And I always thought that if leadership wasn't there, then ultimately you rely on crisis to drive decisions. In the last few years, my biggest concern is that crisis does not seem to drive decisions either.

There is also no guarantee that decisions, even when made during times of crisis, are going to be good ones. A recent account of the evidence concludes that about 80% of fiscal attempts to reduce debt-to-GDP ratios end in failure (Alesina and de Rugy 2013). Especially in recent years, confidence in the political process is low. Fundamental changes to political systems may be needed before economic policies can be put back on the right track but this is also highly unlikely.

The almost annual battles over the *debt ceiling*, also called the *debt limit*, are relatively weak attempts to force fiscal consolidation under the threat of a debt default—a type of crisis the government creates for itself to get something done. The debt ceiling was the result of legislation in the early twentieth century aimed at curbing military spending proposals during the First World War. The ceiling has been consistently raised, despite threats to let debt and interest payments default, to allow for greater government borrowing—so in the end, no crisis.

In January 2023, the USA hit the debt ceiling established in 2021 legislation. House Republicans are threatening to not raise the debt ceiling until new legislation is passed to limit government spending going forward. For the time being, the US Treasury Department cannot issue new debt and is forced to take *extraordinary measures* to fund the government. These measures include shuffling funds across agencies, with extra funds going to those that are short on funds, and temporarily retiring and redeeming government debt held in fully funded pension plans of government workers. The current estimate is that the government can play this shell game until about June. Is the US political environment different enough from the past to cause debt defaults and forced across-the-board spending cuts in the summer of 2023?

Fiscal Reform Suggestions

COVID-19 and the government's stimulus response to it have postponed any chance of long-run fiscal reforms, while at the same time making them more urgent. Some type of economic crisis related to rising interest rates and the ballooning debt will evidently be needed before we see any major policy consolidation. We have seen this play out in the UK during September of 2022 (see Chapter 1). Similar events could happen in the USA. When they happen, here is a summary of the reforms most commonly suggested by economists. In picking the reforms to emphasize, we keep one eye on the other major issues discussed in Chap. 1 and in subsequent chapters. We ignore several interesting policy suggestions to focus on the reforms we believe are most essential and most practical. For example, there are sound arguments for relying more on national consumption taxes than on income taxes, for eliminating Medicare and replacing it with a government-funded medical voucher program, and for converting PAYG social security to a fully funded program.[11] However, these are large and politically controversial reforms that are not likely to lead to the timely changes needed within the next decade to avert or deal with a financial crisis. The more modest reforms we stress will be difficult enough to pass.

[11] See, for example, Kotlikoff and Burns (2012).

Aging and Healthcare Costs

The *demographic transition*, declining fertility and rising life expectancy, is an important stylized fact associated with growing economies. The demographic changes are both the result of and an important cause of economic growth. As economies go through the transition, their economies naturally age. Initially, aging means a smaller fraction of the population is made up of dependent children and a larger fraction of the population is made up of productive workers. However, as the aging continues, the fraction of the working age population begins to fall and the fraction of older retired households begins to rise—forming a group of dependents at the opposite extreme of the age distribution.

Over the course of the twentieth century, the average length-of-life in the USA went from 50 to 78 years. About half of the gain in years was due to those who reached age 60 living longer. The aging is predicted to continue throughout the twenty-first century, continuing long after the Baby Boomers, those born during an uptick in fertility between 1945 and 1965, are gone. As mentioned, it is a general worldwide phenomenon; Europe, Japan, and Russia are aging even faster than the USA.

Aging is changing the world as we know it and, eventually, the government will have no choice but to respond. It was right and noble for societies to provide economic support for the elderly through their governments. In 1970, real Social Security, Medicare, and Medicaid benefits per retiree were less than 40% of per capita income.[12] Currently, these retirement benefits have reached about 75% of per capita income. By the end of the twentieth century, the consumption of retirees began to exceed that of the average worker.[13] The rising consumption of the ever-larger relative population of elderly households is taking up ever-increasing chucks of the nation's income. The trend is unsustainable in an accounting sense. It also is causing national consumption rates to rise and investment rates to fall, contributing to slowing economic growth and widening income inequality. Priority number one is to cap the growth of real retirement benefits to be no faster than real income. Greater real services to the elderly can rise, but no faster than a nation's ability to pay for them.

Aging has created a fiscal issue largely because of the PAYG financing scheme for Medicare and Social Security. The ability to finance retirement programs now depends crucially on the relative size of different age cohorts. Given the growing relative size of the older population, the burden on working households to finance these programs via PAYG financing will only continue to rise. In the USA, there are currently 4.8 workers to support each retiree. By the middle of this century, that number will fall to 2.8. There is concern that the Medicare and Social Security trust funds will both be exhausted within the next 10 years. Benefits will have to be cut or payroll taxes will have to increase.

---

[12] Kotlikoff and Burns (2012 Figure 4.2).

[13] Gokhale et al. (1996).

There was a similar funding shortfall in 1982 that lead to a payroll tax increase, a gradual increase in the age for benefit eligibility, and income taxation of social security benefits.[14] The longer the country waits to bring payroll tax revenues in line with retirement benefits, the more dramatic the changes will have to be, so timing matters. From the perspective of 2015, closing the present value gap between Social Security benefits and taxes would have required a 4 percentage point increase in the current payroll tax rate from 12.4% to 16.4%. Each year that action is delayed, increases the required tax hike. The loss of payroll tax revenue during the pandemic will push the required tax rate calculation yet higher. A more recent estimate of the required rise in the payroll tax is 4.6 percentage points (Goodman and Kotlikoff 2021).

However, it would be best *not* to close the fiscal gap in the Social Security retirement program by raising the payroll tax. Taxing wages would lower saving of working households and hurt economic growth. Instead, the adjustment should be on the benefit side. One commonly proposed solution is to further increase the ages at which one receives the minimum and maximum benefits payout.[15] This solution would increase output and saving by encouraging workers to work longer.[16] If actuaries calculate that this policy change would not close the gap between benefits and taxes, then benefits of higher income households could be cut—which would further encourage private saving among a high saving group.

This combination of policy adjustments would allow both liberals and conservatives to claim victory. Liberals could argue that they saved social security, by keeping the basic structure of the retirement program intact and making it a more progressive. Conservatives could argue that they prevented an increase in the payroll tax on workers. Of course, the policy adjustments would have to take place in the future so that current retirees and those near retirement are not affected.

In principle, the fiscal gap in Social Security should be *relatively* simple to close, in part because it is *relatively* small—a mere 25.8 trillion.[17] In 2015, the Social Security gap was only about 12% of the entire fiscal gap. Much more important contributors to the overall fiscal gap are Medicare and Medicaid, government programs which are predicted to rise the fastest as a share of GDP.[18] For Medicare alone to be rendered solvent requires a 7 percentage point rise in the payroll tax (Goodman and Kotlikoff 2021), again not a policy solution that is consistent with restoring economic growth. As with the Social Security policy adjustments, the new health insurance plan would only apply to those a decade or two away from retirement.

Instead, as mentioned above, the government has no practical choice but to cap the budgets for the health programs so that costs grow no faster than GDP. Kotlikoff

[14] Gokhale (2014, p.77).

[15] Simpson-Bowles Commission (2010), Steuerle (2014), and Alm (2014).

[16] Coile and Gruber (2007), Gruber and Wise (2004), and Gustman and Steinmeier (2015).

[17] Kotlikoff (2015).

[18] Auerbach et al. (2004). Although any significant rise in interest rates would cause debt service to rise faster than health expenditure.

and Burns (2012) recommend that the government's health expenditures be capped at the current 10% of GDP by offering a basic healthcare insurance plan. The coverage under the basic plan would be determined by a healthcare panel that would revise the plan annually to make expenditures consistent with the 10% cap. Limiting the government's subsidy of healthcare should create incentives to limit the quantity of marginally valuable services and to make technological innovations more cost conscious.

The capping of Medicare and Medicaid budgets puts the government in a position where it cannot provide insurance that automatically covers "the best (most expensive) available care." There will certainly be major political and legal hurdles associated with taking this position. The health economist Mark Pauly (2014, p. 36) puts the problem this way, "It is not yet acceptable for middle-class people to talk about anything but the best available care, and legal liability may prevent the emergence even of what they would accept." The government and private insurers must be able to constrain doctor and patient choices without facing lawsuits when expensive procedures and treatments are not covered as pointed out by Kotlikoff and Burns 2012, Chapter 9).

It is not clear that reducing medical expenditures lowers the quality of care. Medical doctors themselves are thinking of ways of reducing the use of costly tests and treatments.[19] We think the middle class, having seen a decline in their ability to buy non-medical goods and services over several decades now, are ready to consider limits on what they continue to spend on healthcare. Improvements in their economic situation from the reforms discussed in future chapters would help households accept a more basic health that they could possibility supplement with their own private insurance. Better informing the public about the fiscal gap, its connection to health expenditures, and the economic consequences of not closing the gap would also be essential.

Improving Tax Compliance

Stemming the growth in the entitlement programs is not sufficient to completely close the fiscal gap. In addition to reducing the path of future spending, more tax revenue will be needed to reduce the creation of government debt that pulls down national saving and investment. Political considerations suggest that higher taxes will almost surely be part of any grand compromise to resolve the fiscal crisis. Beyond the goal of closing the fiscal gap, extra revenue will also be needed to increase public infrastructure investment and funding for basic research—essential government investments that have been neglected. The question is how can tax revenues be increased in a way that eliminates distortions and inequities while minimizing negative growth effects?

[19] Allen (2018) and Gordon (2018).

One way to raise tax revenue is simply to do a better job of collecting the taxes that are owed. Tax compliance refers to the payment of taxes owed under the current tax code. The gap between taxes owed and taxes actually paid in 2019 was $600 billion. Over the next decade, the cumulative tax gap is estimated to total about $7 trillion (roughly 15% of the taxes owed).[20]

President Biden's tax compliance initiative in the proposed American Families Plan legislation seeks to restore the IRS budget, which has been slashed by 20% in the last decade, to provide the IRS with better income tracking information from third parties such as employers and financial institutions, and to regulate the behavior of private tax preparers. The majority of American households support investments to make taxpayers more compliant under the current tax code. Greater IRS funding is now a component of the recent 2022 Inflation Reduction Act.

Removal of Tax Expenditures

Another good place to start raising more tax revenue is to reduce "tax expenditures"—tax exemptions, deductions, credits, and deferrals that lower taxes paid. The US tax code allows for over 150 different tax expenditures. These tax expenditures are large, $1.2 trillion in 2015, larger than government spending under either Medicare and Medicaid programs or the Social Security program. In addition, the vast majority of the expenditures flow to the top 40% of income earners.[21]

The biggest tax expenditure by far is the tax exclusion for health insurance, provided as a form of employee compensation and totaling about $200 billion. This tax exclusion has no sound basis in economic logic. It was created during World War II when employers began competing for scarce workers by offering more attractive benefits because their potential wage offers were frozen by the wage and price controls of the period. The National War Labor Board, as a concession to business, ruled that the benefits were not wages and not subject to wage controls. To maintain consistency, the concession meant benefits should not be treated as taxable income. The health insurance tax exclusion increases the generosity of health insurance, the demand for medical services, and healthcare costs. As with many of the tax expenditures, it is highly regressive because high wage workers benefit the most from the reduction in their taxable income.

Other tax expenditures should also be considered for elimination or reduction. Two of the largest are the reduced tax rate on income from capital gains and the deductibility of mortgage interest on owner-occupied housing, together totaling over 150 billion in lost revenue. These tax expenditures are also regressive, and they likely reduce net national saving used to fund business capital formation.

[20] See data from the Center on Budget and Policy Priorities (2016).

[21] See the US Department of the Treasury (2021).

Tax Rates and Tax Revenue

Some policy makers hesitate to raise the capital gain tax rate because of the belief that a higher rate will translate into *less* tax revenue collected, defeating the debt-reduction purpose. The idea is that a higher tax rate will lower the capital gains realized because the market value of assets will fall and/or because asset holders will become less willing to sell assets, thereby reducing the tax base so much that less revenue will be collected despite the higher tax rate.

For several decades, there have been debates about the empirical effects of capital gains taxation. Economists have not done much to sharpen the debate because econometric estimates of the effects of changing capital gains tax rates vary dramatically, some supporting policy makers' reluctance to raise rates and some opposing it. A recent state-of-the art attempt to provide reliable estimates implies the fear that a high rate will result in lower tax revenue collected is unfounded. Agersnap and Zidar (2021) find that capital gains tax cuts do not "pay for themselves," as is often claimed. Their estimates suggest a 5 percentage point increase, from the current rate of taxation, would yield somewhere between $20 and $30 billion in additional annual federal revenue. They calculate that the revenue maximizing capital gains tax rate is about 40%, far above the current rate of 28% (the average across states including state and federal capital gains tax rates).

The wishful thinking that lowering tax rates can result in more tax revenue goes beyond the taxation of capital gains. The Trump Tax Cuts and Jobs Act in 2017 reduced the federal corporate profit tax rate from 35% to 21%. Since then, one hears many claims that the reduction in rates caused more tax revenue to be collected. Most professional economists, however, have estimated that the investment and output responses that *resulted from the tax cuts* were too weak to generate more revenue. Slemrod and Bakija (2017, Ch.4) survey the taxation literature and conclude that the response of labor supply, saving, and investment to marginal tax rate cuts are far too modest to result in greater tax revenue. They argue that tax revenues over the last 40 years would have been much greater if not for policies that reduced tax rates.

High debt economies are particularly bad ones in which to expect large output and income gains from tax cuts. An interesting recent study by Fotiou et al. (2020) used post-WWII data to estimate the output effects of capital income tax changes *conditional on government debt levels*. The research finds that output effects of capital income tax cuts are highly dependent on the government debt levels at the time of the cuts, with less of an expansionary effect when debt levels are high than when they are low. One reason for this is that markets believe that when debt levels are high, there is likely to be a policy reversal or a future increase in other taxes. This belief would only be rational if markets also believed that the original capital income tax cut meant there was a high probability of additional government borrowing due to a loss in tax revenue collected. The authors also find that as debt ratios move above 100%, there will not only be a loss in tax revenue but a loss in output itself, i.e., the tax cuts will be *contractionary*. We are currently in this debt ratio territory.

Efficiency-Promoting Taxation

As discussed by Mankiw (2009), economists are generally advocates for *Pigovian* taxes. Pigovian taxes are known as corrective taxes because they are taxes that attempt to correct inefficiencies in market resource allocation that result from decision-makers not internalizing the *social* costs, or *negative externalities*, associated with their actions. As with the fiscal crisis, global warming poses a major economic threat to the world in the twenty-first century. Placing a Pigovian tax on carbon emissions would address both crises by creating a revenue source and by forcing households and firms to internalize the full costs of carbon emissions when deciding on production technologies, type of automobile, driving, and electricity use. A tax on gasoline also reduces negative externalities associated with congested roads such as traffic delays and accidents.

Carbon taxation is receiving serious consideration in the negotiations over the climate change component of the American Families Plan. In a later chapter, we discuss climate change and the carbon tax in detail.

Advances in *behavioral* economics are making a case for increasing *sin* taxes. Behavioral economics identifies situations where decision-making deviates from the fully rational calculus of neoclassical economics. An important source of these deviations is a lack of self-discipline. People know that they should save for retirement but have a hard time doing so, especially when retirement is far away. This is one reason why Social Security and corporate pension plans are popular institutions—they force people to do what they know they should do, but often do not because of a lack of will. People also lack discipline in taking care of themselves. Sin taxes are consumption or sales taxes targeted on goods that make us unhealthy, such as alcohol, cigarettes, and fatty and high caloric foods. Taxing these goods raises their costs and discourages unhealthy consumption. For example, Los Angeles County is considering a tax on sugar-sweetened beverages to improve health and reduce the social costs of obesity.[22] Doctors at the Mayo Clinic are pushing for higher sin taxes on alcohol and cigarettes.[23] Gruber and Mullainathan (2005) even find that higher cigarette taxes make smokers *happier* by creating incentives to reduce or eliminate the smoking habit.

The sin taxes on unhealthy behavior can also be viewed as a way of mitigating the *ex ante moral hazard* associated with the provision of health insurance. Ex ante moral hazard is what health economists call the tendency of insured individuals to engage in unhealthy behavior because they do not have to fully pay for the consequences of their actions. Ex ante moral hazard is a controversial concept but several recent studies provide empirical evidence that it does exist.[24]

---

[22] Clarke et al. (2015).

[23] Perry (2013).

[24] See Dave and Kaestner (2006), Stanciole (2008), and Dave et al. (2015). Especially in the USA, there is an obvious opportunity to reduce healthcare costs by eating more nutritious food, losing weight, and exercising more.

Consumption Taxes

If the increased revenue from improving tax compliance, reducing tax expenditures, and levying Pigovian and sin taxes is not sufficient, then a general federal consumption tax, perhaps earmarked for increase public investments in infrastructure and basic research, should be considered.[25] Many economists favor a consumption tax base over an income tax base. A complete reform of the US tax code is too big a task to take on while moving quickly to avert a crisis of confidence, but the addition of a relatively small federal consumption tax may be a possible source of additional revenue needed to close the fiscal gap and avert a full-fledged financial crisis. It would also shift some of the burden of closing the gap to older generations.

One of the reasons economists prefer taxing consumption rather than income is that it reduces the distortionary tax on the return to saving. Higher returns to saving have the potential to raise the rate of saving and increase economic growth. However, there is little evidence that saving rates change significantly when after-tax returns to saving increase.[26] Apart from the issue of taxing interest income, a consumption tax is superior to a *wage* tax if the goal is to lower consumption rather than saving and growth.[27]

Short-Run Effects of Fiscal Consolidation

One of the reasons for delays in dealing with the fiscal gap is the concern that the required cuts in government spending and increases in taxes will cause large negative output effects in the short run by reducing aggregate demand. This concern has inspired research that investigates how the short-run loss in output from fiscal consolidation can be minimized. The research on this topic is closely related to the long tradition in economics of attempting to estimate *fiscal multipliers*—a term grounded in Keynesian economics, where exogenous changes in government spending and tax revenues were thought to have much more than one-for-one effects on output.

The best of the modern research in this area attempts to identify episodes where governments explicitly devise fiscal plans to reduce debt and then estimates the

[25] See, for example, the survey in Stupak and Marples (2016).

[26] You may have noticed the absence of a wealth tax as a way of raising additional revenue. Wealth taxes have proven to raise some difficult measurement and tax compliance issues that limit their ability to raise revenue. Wealth taxes also lump together productive assets that raise worker productivity (physical business capital) with assets that primarily raise a family's lifetime consumption (real estate and homes). Finally, a wealth tax punishes rich philanthropists along with the selfish rich.

[27] For analysis of the difference between consumption and wage taxation, see Ivanyna et al. (2021).

resulting output effects.[28] The identified plans can be categorized as largely tax-based (tax increases) or largely expenditure-based (spending cuts). The consensus of this research is that consolidations based largely on spending cuts tend to be associated with mild and short-lived recessions or no recessions at all. Tax-based consolidations, on the other hand, are followed by large and prolonged recessions.

The difference in the two types of consolidation packages appears to work through very different effects on business confidence and private investment. Business confidence does not fall much after expenditure-based adjustments, promptly recovers, and then actually increases. After tax-based adjustments, business confidence instead falls for several years. As a result, spending cuts are associated with relatively small declines, or even increases, in investment—which is important in avoiding both severe recessions and negative longer-run effects on economic growth.

Summary of Policy Reforms

The broad policy suggestions, which we feel should shape the debate about fiscal reforms, are listed below:

1. Increase the age at which the minimum and maximum Social Security retirement benefits are received.
2. Reduce Social Security benefit levels for higher income individuals.
3. Cap expenditures under Medicare and Medicaid, at the current percentage of GDP, by offering a basic plan of healthcare coverage that is revised annually by a healthcare panel.
4. Increase tax revenue by investing in tax compliance and eliminating tax expenditures starting with the tax exclusion for the health insurance provided as a worker benefit, the reduced tax rate on income from capital gains, and the deductibility of mortgage interest on owner-occupied housing.
5. Increase tax revenue by increasing a variety of Pigovian taxes, sin taxes, and a federal sales tax.
6. Increase budgets for public infrastructure and basic research.
7. For the purpose of minimizing negative effects on output in the short-run, consolidation packages should tend to favor spending cuts over tax increases in reducing the fiscal gap.

Of these recommended reforms, the one where we have seen the most movement is infrastructure spending, as the Infrastructure Investment and Jobs Act passed in 2021. It is not entirely clear how it will be paid for. It involves $550 billion in new infrastructure spending over 10 years, and estimates suggest that 1/2 to 4/5 of the

[28] Romer and Romer (2010), DeVries et al. (2011), Alesina et al. (2015) and Alesina and de Rugy (2013), Alesina et al. (2017).

spending with be debt financed.[29] It should raise economic growth in the medium and long run, but the debt financing will mediate the growth effects to some degree. Any associated rise in wages may help create greater willingness to address the tougher reforms that will need to follow.

The recent 2022 so-called Inflation Reduction Act begins to address rising medical costs and the need to increase tax revenue (via a minimum corporate profit tax and greater IRS tax enforcement). These new policies are at least small steps in the right direction needed to address the fiscal crisis.

Leading up to the 2022 mid-term elections, there are whispers from Republicans that it is time for spending caps on Social Security and Medicare, perhaps by increasing the age limits for eligibility—as we ourselves suggest in reform #1 above. This is a reasonable proposal that in a different time (as mentioned, age limits have been increased before) would result in serious discussion and debate. In the past, a discussion might start with a compromise like, "OK, we will talk about raising age limits if you will back off extending the Trump tax cuts (also quite reasonable)." However, because of our divided times and because many Democrats are quite nervous about their re-election prospects, such a discussion will likely not take place. Instead, Democrats will yell as loud as they can that Republicans are planning to cut your retirement benefits and no progress will be made.[30]

Appendices

Appendix 1

The financing of government pension programs has consequences for the country's physical and intangible capital formation. In a closed economy, the consequences can be seen by using the capital market equilibrium condition that investments must be financed by *national saving* (the sum of private and public saving): *Investment = Private Saving + Public Saving.*

Fully funded pensions are essentially forced saving plans (that households generally like because they are concerned about their own discipline to save rather than

[29] Over 10 years, the CBO estimates $256 billion in new debt, Penn Wharton Budget Model estimates $351 billion, and the Committee for a Responsible Budget estimates $400 billion.

[30] It is important to emphasize that the big fiscal consolidations needed to resolve the fiscal crisis must take place in the Social Security and Medicare programs. Tough changes in these programs are made more difficult by the fact that they are part of *mandatory* government spending and are not part of the annual budget process that deals with *discretionary* spending (such as defense, education, and transportation spending). Discretionary spending is subject to an annual negotiation over the size and allocation of spending in different programs but changes in mandatory programs require special legislative action. The annual budgetary drama that includes terms such as appropriations, omnibus bills, continuing resolutions, government shutdowns, and debt limits, all are related to discretionary spending only. For a discussion of this annual budget process, see Committee for a Responsible Budget (2022b).

consume). Households are taxed and the revenue collected is used to purchase government debt that would otherwise have to be issued to the bond market in hopes of finding a lender. Future retirement benefits are then financed by repayment of principal and interest on the bonds that were purchased by the Social Security Trust Fund on behalf of the tax-paying household. The taxes collected cause private saving to fall dollar-for-dollar because the government pension is a substitute for private saving. However, public saving increases dollar-for-dollar because the taxes collected prevent additional government debt from being issued in the bond market (instead the bonds never hit the market and are held in the Trust Fund). Thus, there is no change in the national savings available for domestic investment. While the assumptions made about households in this description are not likely to be strictly true, a fully funded pension system is also not likely to have major effects on domestic investment.

Under a PAYG system, the same taxes would be collected but, instead of being used to purchase government debt, the funds would be used to pay benefits to *current* retirees. Thus, the fall in private saving would not be offset by a rise in public saving (a decline in government borrowing from the market) and domestic investment would fall. The bonds issued to the market, rather than the Trust Fund, cause funds to be diverted from the financing of domestic investment to financing of the government. Thus, debt held by the Trust Fund does not have the same impact on domestic investment as debt absorbed by the bond market, hence the difference between *total* or *gross* debt and *debt held by the public*.

Appendix 2

To see explicitly what low interest rates imply for debt sustainability requires government budget accounting that identifies the dynamics of debt. The annual government budget constraint can be written as

$$B_{t+1} = (1 + r_t)B_t + PD_t$$

where B represents the stock of outstanding government debt, r is the interest rate on government debt, PD is the primary deficit, and the subscripts refer to a calendar date. We can divide through the budget constraint by current, period t, output to view the fiscal accounting as a share of GDP, as sustainability is typically discussed. Using lower-case variables to denote the GDP share or ratio we then have

$$\left(1 + g_{t+1}\right)b_{t+1} = (1 + r_t)b_t + pd_t$$

or

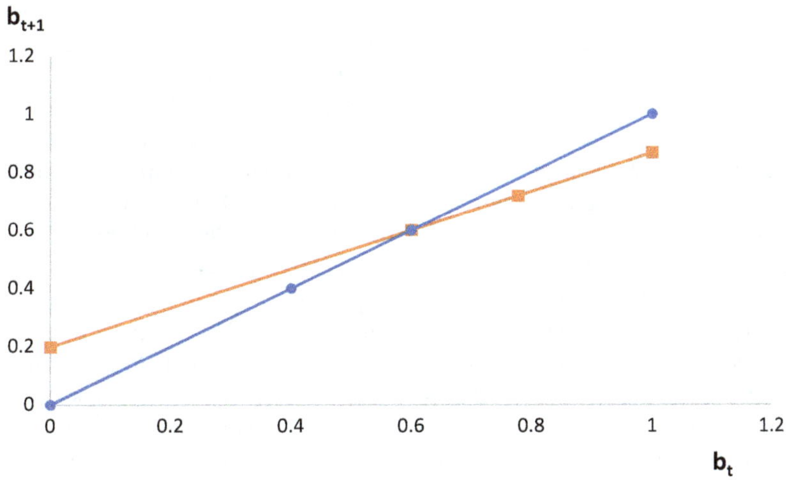

Fig. 2.A Debt dynamics

$$b_{t+1} = \left(\frac{1 + r_t}{1 + g_{t+1}}\right) b_t + \frac{pd_t}{1 + g_{t+1}}$$

where g denotes the growth rate of output and $(1 + g_{t+1})$ is the ratio of output in period t + 1 over output in period t. We can simplify further to make our main points by assuming that the growth rate, interest rate, and primary deficit are constant over time.

A *sustainable debt ratio* is one where $b_{t+1} = b_t = \overline{b}$. First, note that if $r > g$, the only way to sustain a debt ratio $\overline{b}$ is to set policy so that $(g - r)\overline{b} = pd < 0$. That is the government must run a budget surplus indefinitely. This is what the GIBC calls for as well. So in the $r > g$ case, the NPG condition that satisfies the GIBC and sustainability are one and the same.

What happens if $r < g$? In this case our budget equation gives us the following insightful sketch of debt dynamics in Fig. 2.A. Plot b_t on the horizontal axis and b_{t+1} on the vertical axis. The orange line is the budget equation, with slope $(1 + r)/(1 + g) < 1$, and the blue line is the 45-degree line, with slope 1, that bisects the quadrant and is equal-distant from each axis. The numerical form of the debt equation in the plot is $b_{t+1} = 0.6667b_t + 0.20$.

One can trace the dynamics of debt by starting with debt at some point on the horizontal axis, such as $b_0 = 1$, and then going up to the orange budget equation line to find next period's debt value, $b_1 = 0.8667$. The dynamics continue by tracing the value of b_1 horizontally over to the 45-degree line and then down to horizontal axis to establish that the new debt starting point in period 1 is b_1. Then go up to the orange budget constraint line to find $b_2 = 0.7778$ and so on. The value of b will eventually come to rest at $\overline{b} = 0.60$, a *steady state* where starting with the value $\overline{b}$ in one period generates the same value of b in the next period. This $\overline{b}$ value is sustainable.

Notice the sustainable $\overline{b}$ value in the figure is consistent with a constant primary *deficit*, i.e., $pd > 0$, determining the height of the intercept on the vertical axis. The Auerbach-Gale sustainability approach is to target a $\overline{b}$ and then set policies to generate the value of $pd > 0$ that places the budget equation line so as to create a steady state at $\overline{b}$. Polices that generate the pd value in the figure would be sufficient to take the current US b-value at b_0 (say about 100%) down to the targeted value of b at $\overline{b}$ (say 60%). This approach is only possible with $pd > 0$, if r remains below g. If r increases enough to exceed g, then slope of the budget line equation will exceed one, and there will be no steady state b, the debt ratio will just keep rising—so game over (literally, the Ponzi game is over).

Finally, notice that even with $r < g$, sustainability requires *some* policy discipline about the size of pd, which is why Gale (2019) had to work so hard to find the right policy reforms. Currently nothing has been done in the way of reforms; policies have only become more pro-debt and the value of b is rising over time despite $r < g$ (pd is trending upward shifting the budget line equation upward fast enough to offset the favorable dynamics associated with $r < g$).

References

Agersnap, O., and Zidar, O., 2021, "The Tax Elasticity of Capital Gains and Revenue-Maximizing Rates," *American Economic Review: Insights*, 3(4), 399–416.

Alesina, A. and de Rugy, 2013, "Austerity: The Relative Effects of Tax Increases versus Spending Cuts," *Mercatus Research*, George Mason University.

Alesina, A., Barbiero, O., Favero, C., Giavazzi, F., and Paradisi, M., 2017, "The Effects of Fiscal Consolidations: Theory and Evidence," *NBER Working Paper #23385*.

Alesina, A., Favero, C., and Giavazzi, F., 2015, "The Output Effects of Fiscal Consolidation Plans," *Journal of International Economics*, vol. 96, S19–S42.

Allen, M., 2018, "Unnecessary Medical Care: More Common than You Imagine," Shots—*Health News*, National Public Radio.

Alm, J., 2014, "Discussion on Social Security's Financial Outlook and Reforms: An Independent Evaluation," in J. Diamond and G. Zodrow, editors, *Pathways to Fiscal Reform in the United States*, Cambridge, MA: MIT Press.

Alvarez, F., Argenete, D., and Lippi, F., "A Simple Planning Problem for COVID-19 Lockdowns," *Macro Finance Research Program Working Paper* 2020–34, Becker-Friedman Institute: Chicago.

Auerbach, A., 1994, "The US Fiscal Problem: Where We Are, How We Got Here, and Where We Are Going," *NBER Macroeconomics Annual*,9, 141–186.

Auerbach, A., Gale, W., and Krupkin, A., 2018, "The Federal Budget Outlook: We Are Not Winning," *Tax Notes*, July 30:643.

Auerbach, A., Gale, W., and Orszag, A., 2004, "Sources of the Long-Term Fiscal Gap," *Tax Notes*, May, 1049–1059.

Blanchard, O., 2019, "Public Debt and Low Interest Rates," *American Economic Review*, 109 (4), 1197–1229.

Brumm, J., Feng, X., Kotlikoff, L., and Kubler, F., 2021, "When Interest Rates Go Low, Should Public Debt Go High?" Working Paper.

Carnehl, C., Fukudo, S., and Kos, N., 2022, "Epidemics with Behavior," *Journal of Economic Theory* (forthcoming).

CDC, 2022, "CDC Moving Forward Summary Report," *Center for Disease Control and Prevention*: Atlanta.

Center on Budget and Policy Priorities, 2016, "Federal Tax Expenditures," *Policy Basics*, February 23, www.cbpp.org.

Clarke, L., Horst, R., Izuchukwu, K., Lunderville, C., Prasanna, S., 2015, "Reducing Obesity in Los Angeles County: Toward a Tax on Sugar-Sweetened Beverages," *An Applied Policy Project*, UCLA Luskin School of Public Affairs.

Commission for a Responsible Federal Budget, 2022a, *The CRFB Fiscal Blueprint for Reducing Debt and Inflation*, Washington DC, October 26.

———, 2022b, *Q&A: Everything You Should Know about Government Shutdowns,* Washington DC, December 12.

Cochrane, J., 2021, *The Fiscal Theory of the Price Level*, forthcoming.

Coile, C., and Gruber, J., 2007, "Future Social Security Entitlements and the Retirement Decision," *Review of Economics and Statistics*, 89(2), 234–246.

Dave, D. and Kaestner, R., 2006, "Health Insurance and Ex Ante Moral Hazard: Evidence from Medicare," *International Journal of Health Care, Finance, and Economics*, 9, 367–390.

Dave, D., Kaestner, R., and Wehby, G., 2015, "Does Medicaid Coverage for Pregnant Women Affect Prenatal Health Behaviors?" *NBER Working Papers* 21049.

DeVries, P., Guajardo, D., Leigh, D., and Pescatori, A., 2011, "A New Action-based Dataset of Fiscal Consolidation," *IMF Working Paper* 11/128, International Monetary Fund.

Diamond, P., 1965, "National Debt in a Neoclassical Growth Model," *American Economic Review*, 55 (5), 1126–1150.

Di Giovanni, J., Kalemli-Ozcan, S., Silva, A., and Yildirim, M., 2022, "Global Supply Chain Pressures, International Trade, and Inflation," *NBER Working Paper* 30240, Cambridge MA.

Drazen, A., 2000, *Political Economy in Macroeconomics*, Princeton: Princeton University Press.

Fotiou, A., Shen, W., and Yang, S-C., 2020, "The Fiscal State-Dependent Effects of Capital Income Tax Cuts," *Journal of Economic Dynamics and Control*, 117, Article 103860.

Friedman, T., and Mandlebaum, M., 2012, *That Used to be US*, Picodar: New York.

Furceri, D., and Pescatori, A., 2014, "Perspectives on Global Real Interest," Chapter 3 in *World Economic Outlook: Recovery Strengthens, Remains Uneven*, IMF, Washington, DC.

Gale, D., 2019, *Fiscal Therapy*, New York: Oxford University Press.

Gokhale, J., 2014, "Kicking the Social Security Can Down the Road," *Investor's Business Dailey*, August 5.

Goodman, J., and Kotlikoff, L., 2021, "The Really Scary News in the Social Security Trustees Report," *The Hill* 9/25/21.

Gokhale, J., Kotlikoff, L., and Sabelhaus, J., 1996, "Understanding the Postwar Decline in US Saving: A Cohort Analysis," *Brookings Papers on Economic Activity*, 1, 315–390.

Gordon, M., 2018, "Why Do Doctors Overtreat?" *Shots—Health News*, National Public Radio.

Gruber, J., and Johnson, S., 2019, *Jump-Starting America*, New York: Public Affairs.

Gruber, J., and Mullanainthan, S., 2005, "Do Cigarette Taxes Make Smokers Happier?" *B.E. Journal of Economic Analysis and Policy*, 5, 1–45.

Gruber, J., and Wise, D., 2004, *Social Security Programs and Retirement Around the World : Micro-Estimation,* Chicago: University of Chicago Press.

Gustman, A., and Steinmeier, T., 2015, "Behavioral Effects of Social Security Policies on Benefit Claiming: Retirement and Saving," *Journal of Public Economics*, 129, 51–62.

Ivanyna, M., Mourmouras, A., and Rangazas, P., 2021, *The Macroeconomics of Corruption*, New York: Springer.

Kotlikoff, L., 2015, "America's Fiscal Insolvency and its Generational Consequences," Testimony to the Senate Budget Committee.

Kotlikoff, L., and Burns, S., 2012, *The Clash of Generations*, Cambridge, MA: MIT Press.

Mankiw, G., 2009, "Smart Taxes: An Open Invitation to Join the Pigou Club," *Eastern Economic Journal*, 35, 14–23.

Mankiw, G., 2020, "A Skeptics Guide to Modern Monetary Policy," *AEA Papers and Proceedings*, 110, 141–144.

Malinovskaya, A., and Wessel, D., 2017, "The Hutchins Center Explains: Public Investment," *Upfront*, Washington: Brooking Institution.

Pauly, M., 2014, "Medical Spending Reform and the Fiscal Future of the United States," in J. Diamond and G. Zodrow editors, *Pathways to Fiscal Reform in the United States*, Cambridge: MIT Press.

Perry, S., 2013, "Mayo Doctors Propose Higher—and New—"Sin Taxes"," *MinnPost*, June 15.

Rachel, L., and Summers, L., 2019, "On Secular Stagnation in an Industrialized World," *Brookings Papers on Economic Activities*, Spring, 1–54.

Rangazas, P., and Russell, S., 2005, "The Zilcha Criterion for Dynamic Inefficiency," *Economic Theory*, 26, 701–716.

Romer, C., and Romer, D., 2010, "The Macroeconomic Effects of Tax Changes: Estimates using a New Measure of Fiscal Shocks," *American Economic Review*, 100, 763–801.

Saving, T., 2019, *A Century of Federal Reserve Monetary Policy*, Hackensack, NJ: World Scientific.

Simpson-Bowles Commission, 2010, *The Moment of Truth*: Report of the National Commission on Fiscal Responsibility and Reform, Washington DC.

Slemrod, J., and Bakija, J., 2017, *Taxing Ourselves: A Citizen's Guide to the Debate over Taxes* (5th edition), Massachusetts: MIT Press.

Stanciole, A., 2008, "Health Insurance and Lifestyle Choices: Identifying Ex Ante Moral Hazard in the US Market," *Geneva Papers*, 33, 627–644.

Steuerle, C., 2014, *Dean Men Ruling*, New York: Century Foundation Press.

Stupak, J., and Marples, D., 2016, "Consumption Taxes: An Overview," *Congressional Research Service*, 7-5700, www.crs.gov.

US Treasury Department, 2021, "Report on American Families Plan's Tax Compliance Agenda," Press Release May 20.

Wessel, D., 2012, *Red Ink*, New York: Crown Business.

Chapter 3
Human Capital Policy

For most of the twentieth century, the USA experienced several attractive economic trends. There was rapid growth in worker productivity and living standards that were evenly shared across income groups. The US education system pushed most workers through high school and many went on to study at publically subsidized universities. There were fears that the number of new college graduates was *greater* than the market demand for their services.[1] Due to the rapid expansion in college graduates, along with the shared productivity gains for those with less schooling, the excess wage earned by a college graduate compared to a high school graduate actually fell in the middle of the century—a *falling* college or skill premium. In addition, upward mobility was improving as correlations between the incomes of parents and their children became weaker. During the century spanning from 1870 to 1970, education played a significant positive role in generating worker productivity growth and reducing inequality.

Sometime after 1970 things changed. Growth in worker productivity began to slow and gains in real income became concentrated in the top quintile. The fraction of the population graduating from 4-year colleges stagnated. The college premium started to rise and upward mobility weakened. The education system that had served the country so well for a century was no longer making significant contributions to economic growth and income equality.

Growth in years of schooling and days attending school within the year slowed. Standardized test scores stopped rising. The high school dropout rate and sub-functional literacy/numeracy in the workforce remained problematic with little improvement over time. The relative cost of college and student debt exploded, while the standards and quality of college generally fell. After the turn of the twentieth century, "residual" inequality among the highly educated increased as

[1] The concern over an excess of college graduates was discussed in the widely read *Overeducated American* by Richard Freeman (1976). The college wage premium over those with a high school education fell dramatically over the 1970s.

© The Author(s), under exclusive license to Springer Nature Switzerland AG 2023
A. Mourmouras, P. Rangazas, *US Economic Policy in the 21st Century*,
Professional Practice in Governance and Public Organizations,
https://doi.org/10.1007/978-3-031-36437-2_3

only the college graduates in STEM majors or those who went on to graduate school saw gains in real income.

In this chapter we look at the good, bad, and the ugly of education in US history. The historical lessons help to form a critique of the current state of education and suggest what must change for education to once again play a positive economic role. Our suggested reforms place a greater emphasis on pre-school learning, early nutrition, and vocational education that will benefit the majority of the workforce. Fewer, not more, people should be encouraged to attend traditional colleges and the standards for those who do attend should be raised.

The Good

In US history, there was a steady rise in education investment from 1870 to 1970.

1870–1910	Spread of Public Primary Education
1910–1940	Public high school movement
1940–1970	Rise of public universities

Average years of schooling increased by almost 7 years from 1870 to 1970. Days attending school within a school year doubled. Real spending per student increased more than ten-fold. The public was willing to pay for the investments to increase the productivity of the country's workforce.[2]

The schooling investments paid off for the nation. Schooling was an important source of worker productivity growth from 1870 to 1990, causing between 1/5 and 1/3 of the observed rise in worker productivity over 120 years. The investments also served to lower inequality. From 1915 to 1980, the expansion in the supply of college-educated workers outstripped the demand and reduced the extra wage earned by college graduates over high school graduates from 65% to 40%—a declining college wage premium. For more than a century, US education policy was as important as any other single policy in promoting its rise to an economic superpower.

The Bad

Basic economics warns of diminishing returns in all types of investments and productive activities more generally. In the case of education, diminishing returns means it becomes increasingly difficult and expensive to push larger segments of the population through a given level of education and it becomes more difficult for each individual to learn more advanced material. These realities mean that the embodied

[2] See Rangazas (2002) and Goldin and Katz (2008).

knowledge and skills, "human capital," of the average worker cannot grow at the same rate forever. The inevitable slowdown in education attainment after 1970 explains a significant portion of the slowdown in average worker productivity growth that we have been experiencing for 50 years.

It all started with a slowdown in the growth in years of schooling per worker. Consider the increase in average years of school per worker by decade.[3]

Decade Gains in Years of Schooling per Worker

1940–1980	*1980–2005*
0.86	0.43

The gain in years of schooling has fallen to half the pace witnessed during the initial expansion of public universities from 1940 to 1980.

The fall-off in the pace of educational achievement also shows up in years of school by age cohort.[4] Comparing the generation born in 1925 to the generation born in 1950 saw the younger generation with over 2 additional years of schooling. The average worker born in 1925 had fewer years of schooling than what was needed to graduate from high school, while the average worker born in 1950 experienced some college education. Looking ahead toward the gains over the next 25-year generational gap saw schooling rise by less than a year.

Years of Schooling by Birth Year

1925		*1950*		*1975*
10.9		13.2		13.9
	+2.3 years		+0.7 years	

Naturally, the slowdown in average years of schooling is linked to a slowdown in college graduation rates. The 4-year college participation rate for *high school graduates*, age 23 and under, showed little trend from 1970 to 2000—never consistently rising above 60%.[5] College completion rates for the same population group was trendless over the period at about 20% of the age cohort.[6] The numbers have improved little in this century. The 4-year college enrollment rate for *all* those aged 18–24 has been about 30% with a weak upward trend.

College Enrollment Rates (all aged 18–24)

2005	*2015*	*2020*
0.29	0.30	0.31

Six-year college graduation rates, for those attending college this century, have been 60% or less. That means that less than 20% of all those aged 18–24 are completing a 4-year degree.[7]

[3]Goldin and Katz (2008, Table 1.2).

[4]Gordon (2016, p. 513) and Katz (2005, pp. 270–274).

[5]Carneiro and Heckman (2005, Figure 2.2(a)) and Turner (2004, Figure 1.1).

[6]Turner (2004, Figure 1.2).

[7]National Center for Education Statistics (2021, Table 302.10) and Denning et al. (2020).

Lately, it has taken students longer to graduate. Graduation rates have also been measured up to age 30.[8] The age 30 completion rate continued to rise slightly after 1970 but leveled off at about 30% in 2000, significantly above the completion rate by the age of 24. Nevertheless, even extending the time needed to graduate implies that in the USA at most 1/3 of those under 30 have completed a 4-year college degree.

Some of the modest rise in years of schooling is also due to more 18- and 19-year-olds enrolling into 2-year colleges after high school. The percent of 18- to 19-year-olds who have completed high school and are enrolled in some type of college has risen from 60% in 1990 to 66% in 2013 but has not shown much trend since.[9] The six percentage point rise was almost entirely due to increased enrollment in 2-year colleges. The percentage enrolled in 4-year colleges was essentially flat at 40% over this period. After 2013, enrollment rates for 4-year colleges rose slightly before again leveling off, while enrollment rates in 2-year colleges have actually fallen.

Some note that the employment share of those with at least a college degree has risen steadily since 1980 reaching 39% in 2015 (e.g., Valletta 2018). This rise confounds the weak rise in age cohort college graduation with demographic trends. As the US population ages, and the oldest workers retire, the percent with college degrees naturally rises because older workers have lower college graduation rates than younger workers. Another reason the 39% of *employed* workers with college degrees exceeds the under 30 graduation rate of closer to 30% is because the unemployed and individuals who are not in the civilian workforce disproportionately include those without a 4-year degree. As we discuss later in this chapter, a long-run decline in the labor force participation of less than college-educated males, almost 15 percentage points, is one of the reasons for the slowdown in US economic growth (Blinder and Bound 2019; Ullrich 2021).

The Ugly

For most college students, the real cost of college is rising much faster than wages.[10]

Average price of undergraduate degree (inflation-adjusted 2015 dollars)

1987	*2015*	
$39, 643	$103,616	(161% increase)

Average starting salary—First 2 years (inflation-adjusted 2015 dollars)

1987	*2015*	
$49, 406	$50,556	(2.3% increase)

[8] Turner (2004, Figure 1.5).

[9] National Center for Education Statistics (2015, 2021).

[10] Behrman and Zehngebot (2017).

College is not a good investment for many students, and it is not surprising that attendance and graduation have stalled despite a rising college premium. In the USA, from 1980 to 2012, male college graduates with a bachelor's degree experienced an annual rise in real earnings of only 0.5%. To get ahead today, one generally needs a graduate degree. Full-time male workers with a *graduate* degree saw their real earning rise 1.1% annually, not great by historical standards but twice the rate for 4-year college graduates.[11]

The weak real wage gains for college graduates overall can be explained by deteriorating quality of a college degree. This means the modest rise in the years of schooling *overstates* the rise in human capital because all indicators suggest a decline in skills acquired by the average college student.

The problem begins with education before college. The record of college preparedness in the USA is particularly poor for such a rich and highly educated country. On the Program for International Student Assessment (PISA) test, taken by 15-year-olds across 34 OECD countries, the USA ranks 27 in math, 20 in science, and 17 in reading. The relatively poor performance of the USA on the PISA test has not changed over time. Despite rising real expenditures on high school students, national test scores have also been relatively flat for the past 50 years. In fact, the test scores have recently dipped (pre-pandemic) and hit lows that haven't been seen for decades. Only about 40% of high school graduates are deemed prepared for success in college by their performance on the SAT and only 28% by their performance on the ACT.

Schooling is doing no better job in preparing high school students, who do not attend college, for the workplace. Performance on measures of adult skills (basic literacy and numeracy needed for work) has slipped. OECD measures of basic skills peaked for cohorts born between 1978 and 1987 and have fallen since. Among the OECD countries, the recent decline in scores is largest for the USA.[12]

With at best a mediocre and stagnant track record in getting students ready for college, it is not surprising that enrollment and graduation rates are also relatively stagnant. Per pupil spending has risen over time at all levels of education, so the obvious conclusion is that the average marginal returns to human capital investments under current education policy are low.

Given the lack of progress in preparing students for college, it is surprising that grades given in college courses are up. With no indication of an improvement in college preparedness, the rise in grades suggests that standards and content in college are slipping and those who do graduate have fewer skills than in the past. In 1960 about 33% of all grades given were As; today it is 43%. The rise in grades is even more dramatic at prestigious schools. In 1966, Harvard gave 22% As, in 2002 the

[11] See Autor (2014). Blinder and Bound (2019) estimate real wage declines for all education groups except those with graduate degrees from the mid-1970s to the mid-1990s. Wages of four-year college graduates rose in the late 1990s but then largely leveled out, while those with advanced degrees continued to increase modestly.

[12] See Adams (2016) and Hanushek (2005, pp. 252–259) for U.S. SAT scores and Rothwell (2016) for OECD scores of basic workforce skills.

percent of As at Harvard was 46%. The rise in grades coincides with a *decline* in student study time. Students study about 13 h less per week today than in the 1960s.[13]

The only explanation for the combination of flat college preparedness, declining study time, and rising grades is an elimination of course content and a lowering of standards. It is difficult to find older college professors who do not admit to eliminating content and lowering standards over their careers. In fact, it is becoming increasingly difficult to simply find a professor if you look for them in a university classroom. In 1960, 75% of college instructors were full-time tenure track professors. Today the number is 27%.[14]

The fact that the real wages and productivity of college graduates have only weakly increased over time is the ultimate indication of a lack of advanced skill acquisition. As mentioned above, instruction by full-time tenured faculty and student study time have both fallen dramatically over the same period. The human capital associated with a college degree is not what it used to be, but the skills provided to high school graduates are an even worse match for what employers are looking for. Those with some college saw no gain in real wages and those with high school degrees currently receive lower real earnings than they did in 1980. Remember only 30% of each age-cohort eventually complete a 4-year college degree, so the majority of workers have not experienced a rise in real earnings since 1980.[15]

Making of the Public University Corporation

What has caused the cost of a college investment to rise so much faster than income? There is persistent confusion over the role of state funding for public universities as a source of the rising cost of college. Much attention has been given to the idea that *student costs* have risen because universities have been forced to raise tuition to make up for cuts in state funding for higher education. However, the data suggests that cuts in state funding play only a minor role in driving up *college costs*.

First, the evidence for the relationship between tuition costs and state funding is weak. The available empirical estimates reveal relatively small changes in tuition are associated with changes in state funding.[16] Second, it is important to be clear that, for macroeconomic policy assessment, the primary focus should be on *costs* and not *tuition* per se. When talking about determinants of the costs of college to a society, the focus should not be on the *fraction* of those costs covered by student tuition and fees. Regardless of whether the costs are paid for by students or taxpayers, the social costs of college have risen dramatically. The real investment expense to the nation of

[13]Bennett and Wilezol (2013, Chapter 4).

[14]Bennett and Wilezol (2013, p. 139).

[15]Autor (2014).

[16]Delisle (2017).

a college degree has risen and in many cases the return received in enhanced worker productivity is low. Third, looking only at tuition and fees misses the rapid rise in the expense of room and board.[17]

The ability of universities to make the choices that have driven the cost of college higher and the learning component lower is due to an increase in the demand and willingness to pay for college. The increased willingness to pay for college is caused by three forces. First, given the sorry state of high school education and vocational training in particular, a college degree has become an increasingly important requirement for finding a good-paying job. Second, the "college-for-all" mentality has led the federal government to expand financial support for college students from low- and middle-income families.[18] Third, high-income families have come to think of college as the last great consumption experience for adolescences before becoming adult workers.

How is the increased revenue pouring into universities being spent? The rise in spending is not primarily devoted to faculty salaries, as the full-time faculty labor share of the university workforce has been falling for decades. The largest increases in expenditures have little to do with improvement in the substance and delivery of course content. Rather it is based on other components of the university budget that have grown in relative importance. Universities are behaving more like corporations: adding more administrative structure, trying to raise enrollments by responding to student-preferences as consumers, engaging more aggressively in general fund raising, and even stepping up lobbying efforts for government support.

Administrators and their growing support staff have taken up a bigger share of the budget over time.[19]

Administrative Budget is Up

1985–2005 growth in	
Staff	+240%
Administrators	+85%
Students	+56%
Faculty	+50%

Part of the rise is certainly due to increasing government regulation and directives, which should themselves be examined, but part is due to a proliferation of new programs, student activity coordination, counseling, and human resources management. The data we have presented suggests that none of this has increased what students learn in college.

There has also been an increase in college amenities. Less than high-achieving students and students from wealthier families place a large value on campus

[17] Vedder (2019, Figure 10-3).

[18] Gordon and Hedlund (2018), Lucca et al. (2019), and Riegg Cellini and Goldin (2014).

[19] Ginsberg (2011, Table 4). The relative share devoted to administration compared to faculty has continued to grow since Ginsberg's famous report. See, for example, Zywicki and Koopman (2019).

consumption amenities. Universities have been shown to respond to this consumer demand by devoting larger budget shares to amenities.[20]

Universities are turning to professionals to extract their share of tax revenue. Now viewed by university presidents as an essential way to fight for funding and repair the declining public image of higher education, these professionals lobby governments for support. Universities pay for membership in lobbying associations, hire federal relations staff and professional lobbying firms, contribute to election campaigns, and conduct political advertising and student registration drives. The number of higher education associations lobbying in DC doubled over the 20-year period from 1976 to 1996. A motivation for lobbying Washington are the earmarked federal funds for universities—that saw a sevenfold increase over the 1980s. Earmarks for universities by the federal government were eliminated in 2011, but larger universities continue to lobby Washington for research support.[21]

Education and Wage Inequality

Growth in worker productivity via more years of schooling per worker has largely been over for decades, helping to explain the economic growth slowdown. The slowdown in education achievement has another important consequence. From 1950 to 1980, the supply of college graduates increased at about the same pace as the demand for college-educated labor, leaving the relative wage, or *skill premium*, paid to highly educated labor approximately unchanged. Think of the relative demand curve for and the relative supply curve of skilled labor shifting out by equal amounts, leaving the relative market wage paid to skilled labor unchanged (the absolute amount was rising but at the same rate as for workers with less education).

However, as we have previously discussed, the ability of a country to increase its supply of human capital is eventually subject to diminishing returns. Research by Claudia Goldin and Lawrence Katz (2008) quantifies how much skill-biased technological progress raised the relative demand for high-skilled labor over the post-WWII period in the USA. They find that the *demand* for high-skilled labor grew at an approximately constant rate over the historical period. Increases in the relative wage paid to high-skilled labor after 1980 were caused by the degree to which the *supply* of skilled labor was able, or unable, to keep pace with the ongoing demand.

From 1980 to 2005, the skill premium for a college graduate more than doubled. In 1980 a college graduate earned 37% more than a high school graduate. The skill premium rose to 87% by 2005. Valletta (2018) has updated the skill premium estimates. In 2015, the skill premium reached 90%. The rise in wage inequality in the later decades of the twentieth century was caused by the same phenomenon that

[20] Jacob et al. (2018).

[21] On university lobbying, see Cook (1998).

has contributed to the growth slowdown—a decline in the growth of educational achievement.

Given the sharp rise in the college premium during the late twentieth century, one might think the stagnation of college graduation rates would begin to disappear. Why doesn't the high relative wage of college graduates increase college attendance and graduation? As suggested in the previous section, it's because the return to college is not actually high for many graduates and for students who are thinking about attending. The data on this issue is hard to interpret.

Many argue that the average private rate of return for those graduating from college remains high, despite the rapid rise in tuition costs and fees. However, this is at least in part due to a fall in the opportunity costs of attending college, i.e., the forgone wages of high school graduates, have been falling. The opportunity cost of forgone full-time work after high school is the largest part of the cost of college for most students. If a high school education did more to increase productivity and wages, forgone wages would be higher and the average rate of return to college would be lower.

Zimmerman (2014) studies the return to 4-year college for different demographic groups. He finds private returns (based on the subsidized cost to the individual) and social returns (based on the full cost to the society) for male students from poor families are high relative to similar counterparts who attend community college. As with the comparison to a high school education, this could reflect the poor performance and non-trivial costs of community colleges. It is also puzzling why he finds women and students from middle class families attending 4-year colleges do *not* receive higher earnings than their counterparts that attend community colleges. It may be that high schools and community colleges are not benefiting males and students from poor families in particular.

In addition, focusing on the *average* rate of return from a college investment can be misleading. The rates of return vary dramatically for college graduates, with some receiving negative rates of return. Much of the variation in returns to college can be explained by a student's field of study, with STEM majors now significantly outperforming others (Carnevale et al. 2015; Lemieux 2014). The weak rise in wages for many college graduates is revealed in growing wage inequality *among* college graduates.

A general rise in the college premium over high school wages was an important contributor to the rise in overall wage inequality in the late twentieth century. It should be noted, however, that the rise in the college premium was as much due to declining real wages of those without college than to the rise in real wages of college graduates (Binder and Bound 2019, Fig. 1). More recently, the continued rise in wage inequality has been concentrated *within the group of college-educated workers* (Lemieux 2010). This is known as rising "residual" inequality because it cannot be explained by easily observed characteristics such as years of schooling. More than in the past, high returns to college are dependent on the major chosen and whether the student goes on to graduate school or receives on-the-job training (which can be quite extensive in many larger firms).

It is perhaps even more important to note that the rates of return received by *marginal* students and the projected returns to *non-college students*, if they do attended college, can be low even when the *average* return for *graduates* is high.[22] Athreya and Eberly (2013) use the fact that non-completion rates vary substantially with student preparedness and ability in order to explain why many students do not enroll despite the high college premium for college graduates on average. This means it does not make sense to try to push more students through college. In fact, consistent with the significant college dropout rates and the presence of negative returns for some graduates, there may be *too many* students currently attending college.[23]

While the return to college is low for many students and potential students, what's the alternative? Increasingly, middle class households view college as a necessary investment if their children are to have any chance at a decent standard of living in today's world. The USA in particular has a culture that exerts strong social pressure to send children to college, a "college-for-all" mentality.[24] Despite the rising relative cost, about half of each age cohort attends college, but only about one third complete college with a degree in hand.

There is another problem related to the college-for-all mentality at the expense of other human capital investments. We have witnessed not only a rise in inequality but also a drop in intergenerational economic mobility. The correlation between wages of parents and wages of their children increased after 1980.[25] Socioeconomic status of parents is becoming an increasingly important determinant of whether a child graduates from college. Among eighth graders that receive *high* test scores, only 29% graduate from college if their parents are in the bottom socioeconomic quartile, while 74% graduate if their parents are in the top quartile. We agree with Robert Putnam (2015, p. 190) who states, "That last fact is particularly hard to square with the idea at the heart of the American Dream: equality of opportunity." James Heckman (2013, p. 3), the Nobel Prize winning economist, sums up the situation more dramatically:

> The accident of birth is a principal source of inequality in America today. American society is dividing into skilled and unskilled, and the roots of this division lie in early childhood experiences. Kids born in disadvantaged environments are at much greater risk of being unskilled, having low lifetime earnings, and facing a range of personal and social troubles, including poor health, teen pregnancy, and crime. While we celebrate equality of opportunity, we live in a society in which birth is becoming fate.

What options are available to the majority of the nation's households that do not complete a college degree? Their opportunities to earn a decent wage are bleak. This means their children are also not likely to receive the early investments that would give them a good chance at college completion—creating a vicious cycle of

---

[22] Carneiro et al. (2011).

[23] Murray (2008), Kotlikoff and Burns (2012), and Bennett and Wilezol (2013).

[24] Bennett and Wilezol (2013), Hoffman (2011), Murray (2008), and Putnam (2015).

[25] Aaronson and Mazumder (2008) and Davis and Mazumder (2017).

relatively low educational attainment. The problem exists across the developed world but is particularly acute in the USA where over 25% of young workers lack even basic reading and math skills.[26]

Raising the productivity of workers who do not attend college is a challenging task because trends in family structure and falling real incomes for less than highly educated workers are limiting opportunities for children. Then there are those who attend and graduate from college but who are not sufficiently productive to get ahead in today's economy. It is predominately those with graduate degrees and STEM educated undergraduates who are pulling ahead of the majority of workers and widening the spread between the haves and have nots.

Much of the rise in inequality and lack of upward mobility is because the majority of students do not attend or complete college. To get ahead in most developed economies now requires a graduate degree or an undergraduate major that develops quantitative skills. Even college graduation is no longer a guarantee of economic success as evidenced by the rise in "residual" inequality among college graduates during the last two decades.

Other Candidates for Rising Wage Inequality

We argue that wage inequality is predominately due to education inequality. Discussions of rising wage inequality often propose other explanations.

A favorite explanation for the rise in wage inequality is *globalization* and particularly immigration. Chapter 4 discusses the evidence on how globalization has affected US wage inequality in detail. Here we offer a quick summary. While the rise in wage inequality is correlated with the rise in international trade over the last 40 years, this is primarily a coincidence. *Trade* has not been an important causal factor in driving inequality higher. The only significant effect that trade appears to have on the dispersion of wages is based on regional disparities in the concentration of exporting industries and industries facing import competition. The regional disparities have caused a small rise in inequality *within* skill or education groups, contributing to residual inequality. *Offshoring* and global supply chains are on the rise due to increased mobility of physical capital and technology. These trends have the potential to cause job and wage losses in the USA. However, it appears that this is only a minor reason for the rise in wage inequality in the USA due to a contraction in manufacturing jobs for lower skill workers. Finally, surprisingly, there is little or no evidence that *immigration* lowers the wages of native workers across the skill distribution.

The influence of *unions* on the US labor market has declined since the middle of the twentieth century. Union membership as a fraction of the workforce peaked in 1954 at 28% (Mayer 2004). Much of the decline in union membership was during a

[26]Cingano (2014), Corak (2014), Lynch (2005), and Woessman (2015).

period of *declining*, not rising, wage inequality. Given that college and high school educated workers are about equally likely to be union members, one would not expect the decline in union membership to have a significant effect on the rise in the college wage premium after 1980.

A trend decline in the real value of the *minimum wage*, which peaked around 1970, is correlated with the rise in wage inequality. However, less than 10% of the US workforce is directly affected by the minimum wage. For those who are impacted, the effects on income are conflicting because a higher real minimum wage implies job losses for some (Neumark 2018). There is some evidence that a portion of the rise in the wage gap between median workers and those in the bottom decile was due to a declining real minimum wage in the 1980s. Even this measure of inequality has not been impacted by the minimum wage since 1990 (Autor et al. 2016).

Finally, some worry that the rising *market power of large firms* has suppressed worker wages, especially for low-skilled workers. Despite the fears, the evidence is that, holding education constant, workers in larger firms are more productive and receive higher pay than those in other firms (Atkinson and Lind 2018).

Education and the Fiscal Gap

We have seen that deficiencies in formal education have played important roles in slowing economic growth and rising wage inequality. Is there also a role for formal education in creating the fiscal crisis, another of the major economic issues of the century? Yes, indirectly through its impact on economic growth and wage inequality and directly through the creation of the college or bust mentality.

Why has the public allowed the fiscal crisis to develop over several decades? Why has the public tolerated the rise in public debt generally and the delay in responding to the, by now, obvious reality that the social transfer programs are not sustainable into the future? The fiscal situation has become unique in US history. Why now? While surveys indicate growing partisanship, at least since around 2012, surveys also indicated a strong consensus that government budget deficits will hurt future generations and even that fiscal reforms should include spending cuts and tax increases.[27] However, despite these concerns, we have not seen fiscal reforms. Why the continued public acceptance of the policy delays?

The broad middle class must be comfortable with the situation, despite claims to the contrary, because the policies of elected officials suggest an *increased willingness* to burden future generations with public debt. Households are willing to conduct *intergenerational redistribution* when they increase current spending by borrowing and leave the debt for their children to pay. While parents cannot legally do this as individuals, they can do it collectively via the government. Current

[27] Gale (2019, pp. 108–111).

generations of adults feel that their consumption and investment spending is constrained by their lifetime income to be less than optimal and they look to fiscal policy to alleviate the constraint.

The desire to increase household spending beyond the lifetime means of current generations is connected to human capital policy. After more than a century of steady growth, real income for the middle class became stagnant in the 1970s. There have been no real income gains for most of the middle class for over 40 years. The slowdown in worker productivity and wages is partially due to the slower gains in human capital.

At the same time, the importance of advanced education has risen dramatically over time, as indicated by the rising wage premium associated with achieving a college degree. Discretionary household consumption has become increasingly constrained by the lack of real income growth and the rise in the cost of required investments in education. Families wanting to both expand consumption and make the education investments that give their children a chance at success have become increasingly willing to impose a debt burden on their children to help circumvent their lifetime budget constraints.

If more households were experiencing the rise in living standards seen in the middle of the twentieth century, there would be less temptation to burden future generations to expand current spending. The false notion that things will turn around and get better for future generations, without a new policy approach, also plays an important role in encouraging the rising consumption shares of current income. Politicians help to spread the optimistic view of greater future economic growth brought on by an acceleration of technical progress because it relieves them of thinking about the fiscal gap, the poor state of public investment, failed education policy, and climate change.

Better education policies would increase economic growth, reduce wage inequality, and diminish the need for a traditional college education, allowing more households to escape the feeling of being squeezed by falling real income. This, in turn, would create more support for reduced government consumption spending and increased taxation that is necessary to address the fiscal and environmental crises. Raising the standard of living for the broad middle class would improve the country's politics by reducing the temptation to fall for misguided quick fixes to remedy the economic frustration. For this reason, education reform is perhaps more fundamental and pressing than fiscal and environmental reforms.

Technological Progress and Wage Inequality

Economic research has identified another source of the rise in wage inequality—technological progress that benefits high skilled labor, while often substituting for tasks done by low skilled labor. Technological innovations have caused the computer to emerge as an important input in the production of goods and services. College-educated workers have always used the computer on the job to a greater extent than those with less than a college degree, but the gap has increased over time. In 1984 the share of hours worked with a computer was 45.5% for workers with a college degree and 22.1% for workers with less than a college degree. In 2003, these numbers were 85.7 and 45.3, respectively.[28] Computer and information technologies have also led to advances in the sophistication of machines and the automation of production, with "robots" relacing lower skilled labor to a greater degree than higher skilled labor. While these innovations have complemented and raised the productivity of high-skilled labor, they have substituted for and lowered the productivity of lower skilled labor.

A commonly suggested policy response to skill-biased technological change is to devise efficient ways of using taxes and transfers to redistribute some of the gains of high skilled labor toward low skilled labor so as to create a more equitable sharing of the gains from innovation. An alternative strategy is to create skills at pre-college levels of education that enable more workers to benefit from the innovations at the workplace, i.e., to allow the new innovations and lower-skilled labor to *complement* each other in production. At present, skill mismatches and skill shortages exist in many occupations related to the new digital technologies. Robot operators and software engineers are among the skills in short supply. Broad-based vocational education and training must be upgraded to equip the working population with the skills demanded by industry and help workers adapt to automation. A three-way partnership between educational institutions, government, and industry is needed to reexamine core education in high school by strengthening the STEM training and upgrading educational priorities for the digital age. Innovations in technologies and physical capital will benefit young workers if complementarities can be created through vocational training early in life.

The vocational education needed is already taking place in the USA but in an insufficient and piecemeal manner. Some vocational programs at the high school level are currently developing skills that complement the new technologies, for example, programming computer numerical control machines to make plastic molds, training ultrasound technicians to do diagnostic medical imaging, mastering the software commonly used to do business accounting and human resource management, designing and repairing robots that perform a variety of tasks, and understanding advanced equipment that provide power via pressurized air, gas, and water.[29] Models for how we can make progress in increasing worker productivity and wages of those without 4-year college degree exist but they are severely underutilized and underfunded.

[28] Helpman (2018, p. 86).

[29] Newman and Winston (2016, pp. 102–106).

Education Deniers

While we are critical of the current investment *allocation* across different types of education, we do believe that serious education at all levels is an *investment* that has the potential to create useful skills and enhance worker productivity. There are those who are much harsher critics of formal education, considering it more a form of consumption or, at best, a massively wasteful way to signal innate ability (see, for example, Caplan 2018).

There is no denying a strong *correlation* between years of schooling, productivity, and earnings—both across individuals and countries. We believe that this reflects, in part, the accumulation of basic essential skills (numeracy and literacy) as well as more advanced skills and knowledge that improve job performance. One type of evidence supporting this belief is the typical development patterns of a country over the course of history.

Annual values for worker productivity growth rates follow a "hump-shaped" pattern, first rising, then leveling off for many decades, before falling (Gordon 2016). Schooling and school spending per pupil rise slowly before accelerating rapidly and then leveling off, similar to growth rates (Rangazas 2002; Lord and Rangazas 2006). Fertility stays high in early development, sometimes even rising, before it follows a strong downward trend (Galor 2011). The only quantitatively documented explanation that simultaneously matches all these development patterns assumes education has a *causal* effect on worker productivity (Galor 2011; Das et al. 2018).

At the microeconomic level, consider the earnings of college graduates in the market today. If education achievement predominately signals ability rather than acquired skills, it is hard to explain the vast differences in market wages earned by college graduates across majors (Carnevale et al. 2015). Are the graduates in top-earning majors of engineering, computer science, and information technology innately smarter than students in pure mathematics, philosophy, and chemistry, or have they acquired skills and background knowledge that are more useful in expanding occupations?

Throughout US history, the public has supported taxes to provide and improve schools because they believed that students would gain skills and become more productive workers. This started in a world where households were far from rich and agriculture was the dominant sector, continued during the shift to manufacturing, and then through the transition toward the service economy. There are limits to the support for education, as there should be. Diminishing returns are associated with all types of investment. Students and taxpayers should question the high cost of college. But this is because a good thing has gone too far, not because after more than 100 years of increasing the fraction of income spent on education, everyone woke up and realized it was all a waste.

Education and Labor Force Participation

Overall labor force participation has experienced a trend decline in the USA for several decades. While aging certainly has contributed to the decline, as older people naturally participate less than younger people on average, most of the decline is due to a drop in participation of workers aged 16–54 (Abraham and Kearney 2020). Less educated males aged 25–54 stand out in this regard as they have seen dramatic trend declines since 1970; about 12 percentage points for high school graduates and 15 percentage points for high school dropouts.

There is no agreement on the most important explanations for the decline in participation. Blinder and Bound (2019) believe the reasons work through family-related factors that have shifted the labor *supply* of less educated workers to the left. The marriage rate for less-educated males between 25 and 54 has fallen to about half the rate in the 1970s, while the fraction of this group living with at least one parent has more than doubled. Abraham and Kearney (2020) favor forces that have shifted the *demand* for less skilled labor to the left, with the prime candidates being import competition from China and the penetration of automation and robots into the labor market. However, estimates of labor supply elasticities suggest these demand curve shifts cannot be the main drivers. In addition, the negative effects of trade with China on manufacturing employment in lower wage regions abated after 2007, while the participation of less-educated workers has continued to decline. Wu (2022) provides evidence that it is the decline in the *relative* wages of less educated male workers that undermines their social status and willingness to work. The common thread in these explanations is that less-educated workers increasingly lack the productive skills needed to create attractive employment opportunities.

Human Capital Policy Reforms

Our existing approach to education served us well for more than 100 years. It is no longer working as we encounter diminishing returns on the types of investments we have been emphasizing. We need an entirely different approach to human capital investment. The new approach must be guided by the evidence generated over the last 50 years and must also realistically consider the funding constraints facing an aging society during a fiscal crisis. Hard choices must be made about how our education budgets will be allocated.

The idea of pushing everyone through college is not working for the majority of the population. A smaller, not larger, fraction of the workforce should attend traditional colleges that focus on academic training. There should be four pongs to the new human capital growth strategy. First, an expansion in early pre-school investments, especially in disadvantaged households. This will improve young children's health, cognitive skills, and social behavior, providing a basis for success regardless of their education path later during adolescence. Second, a real choice must be provided to families by introducing a socially acceptable and attractive vocational alternative to the traditional focus on academic learning during adolescence. Vocational skills acquired in improved high school programs can create immediate job opportunities with above average pay. Third, so as not to worsen our unsustainable fiscal stance, funds that have been allocated to support college preparation and university education must be reallocated to help finance early childhood investments and vocational education. Finally, for those interested in advanced academic training at the college level, the standards must be raised with a greater emphasis placed on both quantitative skills and a rigorously analytical understanding of human interactions.

Pre-school Investments

The effects of two important types of early childhood investments have been empirically examined in the last 20 years—health and education. Both investments increase a child's chances of success whether they follow an academic or vocational path later in life. We focus first on the effects of early health investments and then move to parental and public pre-school education.

In a large sample of children from disadvantaged households in India, Attanasio et al. (2020c) show that stunting in children ages 0–5 generates *permanent* deficits in both health and cognition, supporting previous research that reached similar conclusions. The result suggests that early interventions related to health and nutrition of infants can have important life-long impacts on worker productivity.

Two recent US studies confirm the lesson from the Indian data within the context of already established government programs. Hoynes et al. (2016) find that access to Food Stamps in utero and up to age 5 improves several long-term health outcomes. For women, family access to Food Stamps during their childhood was shown to raise education and economic outcomes as well. Brown et al. (2020) find greater Medicaid eligibility for families increases college enrollment and decreases fertility for their children. Wages are also higher but are statistically significant only for women. The study traces the children into adulthood, over the ages 19 to 28, confirming that they pay more taxes due to their higher wages. Despite covering only a short segment of the adult work life, the authors compute the present value of the increased taxes collected pays for 58% of the greater childhood Medicaid expenditures. This calculation implies the present value of the *total pre-tax* wage gains are much greater in present value than the medical investments made. Interventions more specifically targeted to young children, than are Food Stamps and Medicaid, would likely be even more cost-effective at raising future adult productivity.

Pre-school educational investments have been subject to very rigorous empirical evaluation in the last 20 years. Two famous programs for disadvantaged children, the Perry and Abecedarian Projects, have been shown to yield average social rates of return in the 6–14% range, certainly higher than the returns received by many marginal college students and the returns from traditional college-prep spending in high schools of middle- and high-income communities.[30] These programs are small-scale in terms of participants and that has raised issues about whether they could be replicated at a state or national level. However, careful studies of large-scale pre-school programs, including Head Start, have also shown the potential to yield benefits.[31]

The designs of large-scale projects such as Head Start differ significantly by location and as a consequence have a fairly wide variation in outcomes. The uneven success of Head Start has given rise to criticisms of the government-funded program. A common feature of the more successful programs, large and small, is a home visit component that educates and encourages parents to stimulate child development at home. Another characteristic of large-scale programs is that the effects on test scores often experience "fade out"—the improvement in scores weaken as the child ages. However, positive effects on behavior, graduation, health, avoiding involvement in crime, and ultimately adult wages tend to be long-lasting.[32]

In the USA, there is currently a range of uncoordinated early-education programs, but the overall funding is low: less than 0.2% of GDP compared to 0.7% in other developed countries (Learning Policy Institute 2021). Just 54% of 3-and 4-year-olds participate in pre-school. Only 5% of 3-year-olds attend a publicly funded pre-K program (Cascio 2018). This is another policy deficiency that is hard to explain because a strong majority of households favor public support for pre-school education.

The original *Build Back Better* program proposed by the Biden administration included almost $400 billion of federal support for childcare and early education. However, this component of the bill was a causality of the dramatic downsizing that resulted in the Infrastructure Investment and Jobs Act 2021. Some momentum for pre-school funding remains in several separate and smaller proposals (Haywood 2022).

In summary, there is growing evidence of high returns to early investment in children from disadvantaged family backgrounds. The fact that the returns to pre-school investment in children from low-income families are higher than the returns to marginal public school spending in middle and upper class neighborhoods suggests that a reallocation of public funding toward early investments in health and learning will increase growth and reduce inequality.

In locations where there are existing pre-school options, disadvantaged households should receive vouchers that allow them to afford the center of their choice. This would help promote competition across centers and may satisfy some of the complaints by critics of Head Start. Vouchers also allow children from lower-income

[30]Heckman et al. (2010), Heckman et al. (2013), and Garcia et al. (2019).

[31]Ludwig and Miller (2007), Deming (2009), Walters (2015), Attanasio et al. (2020a, b).

[32]Disappointing outcomes for some Head Start centers are due to mismanagement, the availability of alternative centers that raise the performance of children in the "control" group, and because of a concentration of children with poor health (reinforcing the importance of early interventions in *both* education and health). See the discussion in Heckman (2013).

families to attend pre-school with children from middle-class families. Evidence suggests that disadvantaged children benefit more when attending pre-schools with middle-class children than when attending schools that are segregated by socioeconomic status (Cascio 2023).

In rural areas without convenient existing programs, centers could be established within local primary schools. At a minimum, any pre-school program should include weekly instructional home visits for families with young children, a proven component of empirically evaluated programs. Given the long-run importance of early childhood health, it is also important that pre-school centers be equipped with primary care medical services and provide nutritious meals. A primary care assistant should accompany the social worker on home visits to discuss nutritious diets and sound health practices.

Vocational Training

Most students who attend college are looking for specific skills that make them attractive to employers and not the more general knowledge and abstract analytical skills that a 4-year college education has traditionally offered. A common frustration among college students is that they are forced to learn material that is of no practical, i.e., job-related, importance. Despite all the social pressures to become "highly educated," college is not the answer for majority of young people who either do not graduate from college or who are disappointed with the lack of job-specific skills they have acquired upon graduation.

Vocational training is an integral component of human capital policy in most European countries but has been neglected and even stigmatized in others. The USA, in particular, needs a cultural shift away from the notion that traditional college is for everyone. Students who want to learn a trade should be respected, and their education should be taken seriously in high school. Social pressure to send most students through a "college-track" program leaves too many students with few practical skills when they enter the workforce after high school.

As with pre-school investments, vocational programs have been shown to have high returns. Perhaps the leading study was a randomized controlled trial targeting disadvantaged urban youth in the USA by Kemple and Willner (2008). The study showed significantly higher earnings after graduation for those randomly assigned to receive greater vocational training during their years of secondary education.

Despite the results of this statistically sound study, there remain doubts about the long-term benefits of vocational education. Critics argue that students who concentrate on vocational education cut themselves off from the general learning that make it easier for them to adapt to technological change or go on to higher education. Descriptive statistics suggest that while students with vocational secondary education initially receive higher wages than those with general education, the advantage reverses itself over time. In addition, those who voluntarily enter vocational education may simply have greater practical aptitude that would result in higher initial wages without the instruction received in vocational classes.

These concerns have been recently addressed by well-designed statistical studies that control for self-selection into vocational programs. Studies of students attending stand-alone vocational schools in Massachusetts and Connecticut found that, relative to comparable peers in traditional high schools, they not only had higher post-graduation earnings but also had higher graduation rates and similar performance on academic tests.[33] While useful for addressing self-selection bias, these studies do not address the possibility that pursuing vocational training over general training may actually lower wages *later* in adulthood.

The possibility that the relative advantage of vocational education may disappear later in life has been examined using data from Norway and Finland.[34] These studies not only control for self-selection but also are able to compare longer-term wage effects lasting into the mid-30s, well more than a decade after graduation. They find a persistent wage advantage for vocational program participants, compared to comparable peers who did not participate, with no evidence of a decline the size of the advantage.[35]

Finally, there is also evidence that vocational programs can be successful in raising the productivity of young adults after their secondary education is over. Attanasio et al. (2017) conduct a randomized controlled study of a vocational training program in Colombia that targeted disadvantaged young adults ages 18–25. They find that those in the program earned higher wages several years after the program ended. They estimate the rate of return on income invested in the program was at least 10%.

The US federal government has a long history of supporting vocational education at the secondary level and postsecondary level dating back to the Smith-Hughes Act of 1917. The support expanded with the Vocational Education Act of 1963 and then, through a series of revisions, became the Carl D. Perkins Vocational Education Act that was first passed in 1984. This legislation provided grants to states to support vocational education in a variety of ways.

However, the size of the support was never very large. The appropriations for the latest iteration 1984, Perkins V, were less than $1.4 billion, a small fraction of the total federal education spending, which exceeds $200 billion. From 1990 to 2010, there are a decline in vocational or what is now often referred to as Career and Technical Education (CTE) credits earned by secondary students.[36] Since 2010,

[33] Dougherty (2018) and Brunner et al. (2021).

[34] Bertrand et al. (2019) and Silliman and Virtanen (2021).

[35] It should be noted that a general theme of all of the studies is that the vocational programs have clear wage advantages for male participants but not necessarily for females. There is some indication that this is because of the fields of study chosen by male and females, with males choosing building and trades and females choosing services.

[36] See Jacob (2017).

there has been a resurgence of local and state interest in CTE but with no significant push in emphasis at the federal level.

The lack of a national push for CTE is surprising because skills that do not require a college education are in short supply in the USA—including carpenters, electricians, technicians, welders, sales representatives, and restaurant staff.[37] These "middle-skill" jobs, which require only quality vocational training in high school (perhaps supplemented with apprenticeships), are among the fastest growing occupations.[38] They are also occupations with relatively high pay. Machine operators make $60,000 annually; technicians, drafters, and respiratory therapists make $70,000; and petrochemical workers make $100,000. In contrast, college graduates in liberal arts and general education make $37,000. Properly designed vocational programs would benefit the majority of students left behind by our fixation on traditional college, leading to greater worker productivity, reduced wage inequality, and increased willingness to address the fiscal crisis.

Less Funding and Higher Standards in Public Universities

The expansion of universities for most of the twentieth century contributed significantly to rising worker productivity. Over the last 50 years, cohort graduation rates have stalled and much of the investments in the education associated with 4-year college degrees have ceased being an important driver of further economic growth. It was tempting to believe that pushing everyone through college was a reasonable goal, but it has not worked. The USA has reached an obvious limit to expanding human capital via its strategy of college for all.

Marginal resources currently devoted to universities should be reallocated to neglected but high-return investments in pre-school children from poor and middle-income families and in high school vocational education that would better serve most students. Refocusing investments to serve most children and adolescents will be a more efficient and equitable use of our scarce education dollars. The evidence also suggests that such a reallocation will result in higher average worker productivity and reduced wage inequality.

Of course, universities will continue to be an important part of sound human capital policy. However, universities need to stop trying to be all things to all people. Instead, the focus needs to be on students who welcome learning abstract and general knowledge. That is what universities were designed to do. They provide highly technical specialized training in important STEM areas. They provide future leaders in business, government, and nonprofits with the broad education needed to

---

[37] For labor shortages in occupations not requiring a college education, see Coster (2010), Duncan (2017), and Collins (2018).

[38] See Duncan (2017), Holzer and Lerman (2009), Lerman (2012), and Newman and Winston (2016).

understand human behavior, society, and the world. Universities should play to their strengths, albeit to a smaller audience and with a renewed degree of rigor, so that most college graduates will benefit from the significant personal and social investment in higher education.

Student Loan Forgiveness?

One new education policy we do not support is student loan forgiveness. The Biden-Harris administration recently announced a unilateral decision to forgive outstanding federally issued student debt obligations for individuals making less than $125,000 and married couples making $250,000. The magnitude of the loss in federal revenue is large, at least half a trillion dollars.

The program is inherently unfair to those who have or will pay off their student loans without the windfall aid. It is also a predominately regressive policy. The income threshold for those who currently hold student loan debt is well above the median household income of about $68,000. It is estimated that less than 40% of the aid will go to households in the bottom two income quintiles, with most of aid going to households in the top three quintiles. Then there is the issue of intergenerational equity. The lost government revenue from loan repayment will be financed by an increase in government debt and greater tax obligations for future generations of workers across the income distribution.

The program is essentially an income transfer that supports consumption spending as it reduces the need of the receiving households to save by retiring their student debt. With inflation rates above 8% in 2022, it is not a good time for the government to be supporting greater consumption.

The worst part of the policy is the opportunity cost of the public funds. The funds lost from loan forgiveness could have been devoted to pre-school programs and vocational training initiatives in disadvantaged areas. These programs would have done much more to reduce income inequality and promote economic growth, while doing less damage to the government's long-term fiscal shortfall.

Summary of Reforms to Human Capital Policy

1. Reduce public funding for undergraduate higher education.
2. Use public funding saved by cutting support for undergraduate higher education to expand public investment in pre-school programs for lower- and middle-income families.
3. Reallocate funds for most high school students away from college-prep to promote a vastly improved vocational track.

4. Raise standards of undergraduate education with a primary focus on STEM areas and a rigorous liberal arts education designed for future leaders in business, government, and nonprofits sectors.

References

Aaronson, D., and Mazumder, B., 2008, "Intergenerational Economic Mobility in the U.S., 1940–2000," *Journal of Human Resources*, 43, 139–172.

Abraham, K., and Kearney, M., 2020, "Explaining the Decline in the US Employment-to-Population Ratio: A Review of the Evidence," *Journal of Economic Literature*, 58, 585–643.

Adams, C., 2016, "2015 SAT, ACT Suggest that Many Students are not College-Ready," *Education Week*, 35 (3), 6

Athrey, K., and Eberly, J., 2013, "The Supply of College-Educated Workers: The Role of College Premia, College Costs, and Risks," *Working Paper* 13–2, Federal Reserve Bank of Richmond.

Atkinson, R., and Lind, M., 2018, *Big is Beautiful: Debunking the Myth of Small Business*, MIT Press: Cambridge MA.

Attanasio, O., Cattan, S., Fitzsimons, E., and Meghir, C., and Rubio-Codina, M., 2020a, "Estimating the production Function for Human Capital: Results from a Randomized Controlled Trial in Columbia," American Economic Review, 110, 48–85

Attanasio, O., Sylva, S., Warrinier, N., Luo, R., Medina, A., and Rozelle, S., 2020b, "From Quantity to Quality: Delivering a Home-Based Parenting Intervention through China's Family Planning Cadres, *Economic Journal* (forthcoming)

Attanasio, O., Meghir, C., and Nix, E., 2020c, "Human Capital Development and Parent Investment in India," *Review of Economic Studies*, 87, 2511–2544.

Attanasio, O., Guarin, A., Medina, C., and Meghir, C., 2017, "Vocational Training for Disadvantaged Youth in Columbia: A Long-Term Follow-up," *American Economic Journals: Applied Economics*, 9, 131–143.

Autor, D., 2014, "Skills, Education, and the Rise in Earnings Inequality among the Other 99 Percent," *Science*, 344, 843–851.

Autor, D., Manning, A., and Smith, C., 2016, "The Contribution of the Minimum Wage to US Wage Inequality over Three Decades: A Reassessment," *American Economic Journal: Applied Economics*, 8(1), 58–99.

Behrman, J., and Zehngebot, J., 2017, "Paying for your College, 30 Years Ago v. Today," *Market Watch*, November 21.

Bennett, W. and Wilezol, D., 2013, "*Is College Worth It*," Nashville, Tennessee: Thomas Nelson.

Bertrand, M., Mogstad, M., and Mountjoy, J., 2019, "Improving Educational Pathways to Social Mobility: Evidence from Norway's Reform 94," NBER WP 25679, Cambridge, MA: National Bureau of Economic Research

Blinder, A., and Bound, J, 2019, "The Decline in the Labor Market Prospects of Less Educated Men," *Journal of Economic Perspectives*, 33(2), 163–190.

Brown, D., and Kowalski, A., 2020, "Long-term Impacts of Childhood Medicaid Expansions on Outcomes in Adulthood," *Review of Economic Studies*, 87, 792–821.

Brunner, E., Dougherty, S., and Ross, S., 2021, "The Effects of Career and Technical Education: Evidence from the Connecticut Technical High School System," NBER WP 28790, Cambridge, MA: National Bureau of Economic Research.

Caplan, B., 2018, *The Case Against Education: Why the Education System is a Waste of Time and Money*, Princeton NJ: Princeton University Press.

Carnevale, A., Cheah, B., and Hanson, A., 2015, *The Economic Value of College Majors*, McCourt School of Public Policy, Georgetown University.

Carneiro, P., and Heckman, J., 2005, "Human Capital Policy," in J. Heckman and A. Kreuger *Inequality in America*, Cambridge MA: MIT Press.

Carneiro, P., Heckman, J., and Vytlacil, E., 2011, "Estimating the Marginal Returns to Education," *American Economic Review*, 101, 2754–2781.

Cascio, E., 2023, "Does Universal Preschool Hit the Target," *Journal of Human Resources*, 58(1), 1–42.

———., 2018, "Why Early Education Matters and Why We Should Pay for It," *Milken Institute Review*, July 31.

Cingano, F., 2014, "Trends in Income Inequality and Its Impact on Economic Growth," OECD Social, Employment, and Migration Working Papers, No.163, Paris: OECD Publishing.

Collins, C., 2018, "My Advice for High School Graduates: Learn a Trade," May 2, otherwords.org.

Cook, C., 1998, *Lobbying for Higher Education*, Nashville: Vanderbilt University Press.

Corak, M., 2014, "Income Inequality, Equality of Opportunity, and Intergenerational Mobility," *Journal of Economic Perspectives*, 27, 79–102.

Coster, H., 2010, "The 10 Hardest Jobs to Fill in America, *Forbes* 5/28.

Das, S., Mourmouras, A., and Rangazas, P., 2018, *Economic Growth and Development*, New York: Springer.

Davis, J., and Mazumder, B., 2017, "The Decline in Intergenerational Mobility after 1980," WP 2017–05, Federal Reverse Bank of Chicago, Il.

Delisle, J., 2017, "The Disincentive Hypothesis : Don't Blame State Budgets Cuts for Rising Tuition at Public Universities," *Report*, Washington: Brooking Institution.

Deming, D., 2009, "Early Childhood Intervention and Life-Cycle Skill Development from Head Start," *American Economic Journal: Applied Economics*, 1, 111–134.

Denning, J., Eide, E., Mumford, K., Patterson, R., and Warrick, M., 2020, "Why have College Completion Rates Increased? An Analysis of Rising Grades," *NBER* Education 2019 Spring Meetings.

Dougherty, S., 2018, "The Effects of Career and Technical Education on Human Capital Accumulation: Causal Evidence from Massachusetts," *Education Finance and Policy*, 119–148.

Duncan, A., 2017, "Education Equality and Excellence will Drive a Strong Economy," *Brown Center Chalkboard*, Washington: Brookings Institution.

Freeman, R., 1976, *The Overeducated American*, Cambridge, MA: Academic Press.

Gale, D., 2019, *Fiscal Therapy*, New York: Oxford University Press.

Galor, O., 2011, *Unified Growth Theory*, Princeton NJ: Princeton University Press.

Garcia, J., Heckman, J., Leaf, D., and Prados, M., 2019, "Quantifying the Life-Cycle Benefits of an Influential Early Childhood Program," *Journal of Political Economy*, 120, 2502–2541.

Ginsberg, B., 2011, *Fall of the Faculty*, New York: Oxford University Press.

Goldin, C., and Katz, L., 2008, *The Race Between Education and Technology*, Cambridge, MA: Harvard University Press.

Gordon, R., 2016, *The Rise and Fall of American Growth: The U.S. Standard of Living since the Civil War*, Princeton: Princeton University Press.

Gordon, G., and Hedlund, A., 2018, "Accounting for the Rise in College Tuition," in C. Hulten and V. Ramey editors. *Education, Skills, and Technological Change: Implications for the Future*, Chicago: University of Chicago Press.

Hanushek, E., 2005, "Comments," in J. Heckman and A. Krueger *Inequality in America*, Cambridge MA: MIT Press.

Haywood, A. 2022, "How to Salvage Federal Funding for Childcare and Early Education," *FutureEd*, October 17.

Heckman, J., 2013, *Giving Kids a Fair Chance*, Cambridge MA: MIT Press.

Heckman, J, Moon, S., Pinto, R., Savelyev, P., and Yavitz, 2010, "The Rate of Return to the HighScope Perry Preschool Program," *Journal of Public Economics*, 94, 114–129.

Heckman, J., Pinto, R., and Savelyev, P., 2013, "Understanding the Mechanisms Through Which an Influential Early Childhood Program Boosted Adult Outcomes," *American Economic Review*, 103, 2052–2086.

Helpman, E., 2018, *Globalization and Inequality*, Cambridge, MA: Harvard University Press

Hoffman, N., 2011, *Schooling in the Workplace*, Cambridge, MA: Harvard University Press.

Holzer, H., and Lerman, R., 2009, "The Future of Middle-Skill Jobs," CCF Brief #41, Center for Children and Families, Washington: Brookings Institution.

Hoynes, H., Whitmore Schanzenbach, D., and Almond, D., 2016, "Long-run Impacts of Childhood Access to the Saftey Net," *American Economic Review*, 106, 903–934.

Jacob, B, 2017, "What We Know about Career and Technical Education in High School," *Brookings Report*, October 5.

Jacob, B., McCall, B., and Stange, K., 2018, "College as Country Club: Do Colleges Cater to Student Preference for Consumption," *Journal of Labor Economics*, 36, 309–348.

Katz, L., 2005, "Comments ," in J. Heckman and A. Krueger *Inequality in America*, Cambridge MA: MIT Press.

Kemple, J. and Willner, J., 2008, "Career Academies: Long-term Impacts on Labor Market Outcomes, Educational Attainment, and Transitions to Adulthood," New York: MDRV.

Kotlikoff, L., and Burns, S., 2012, *The Clash of Generations*, Cambridge, MA: MIT Press

Learning Policy Institute, 2021, "Building a National Early Childhood Education System that Works," *Brief*, March 4.

Lemieux, T., 2010, "What Do We Really Know about Changes in Wage Inequality," in K. Abraham, M. Harper, and J. Spletzer (eds.), *Labor in the New Economy*, University of Chicago Press, 17–59.

Lemieux, T., 2014, "Occupations, Fields of Study, and Returns to Education," *Canadian Journal of Economics*, 47, 1047–1078.

Lerman, R., 2012, "Can the U.S. Expand Apprenticeships? Lessons from Experience, IZA Policy Paper #46.

Lord, W. and Rangazas, P., 2006, "Fertility and Development: The Roles of Schooling and Family Production," *Journal of Economic Growth*, 11, 229–261.

Lucca, D., Nadauls, T., and Shen, K., 2019, "Credit Supply and the Rise in College Tuition: Evidence from the Expansion in Student Aid Programs" *Review of Financial Studies*, 32, 423–466.

Ludwig, J., and Miller, D., 2007, "Does Head Start Improve Children's Life Chances: Evidence from a Discontinuity Design," *Quarterly Journal of Economics*, 122, 159–208.

Lynch, L., 2005, "Comments," in J. Heckman and A. Krueger *Inequality in America*, Cambridge, MA: MIT Press.

Mayer, G., 2004, "Union Membership Trends in the United States," *Congressional Research Report for Congress*, Library of Congress: Washington DC.

Murray, C., 2008, *Real Education*, New York: Three Rivers Press.

National Center for Education Statistics, 2021, College Enrollment Rates and Immediate College Enrollments Rates, *The Condition of Education*, Washington DC.

———, 2015, College Enrollment Rates and Immediate College Enrollments Rates, *The Condition of Education*, Washington DC.

Neumark, D., 2018, "Employment Effects of Minimum Wages," *IZA World of Labor*.

Newman, K. and Winston, H., 2016, *Reskilling America: Learning to Labor in the Twenty-First Century*, Metropolitan Books: New York.

Putnam, R., 2015, *Our Kids*, New York: Simon and Schuster.

Rangazas, P., 2002, "The Quantity and Quality of Schooling and U.S. Labor Productivity Growth (1870–2000), *Review of Economic Dynamics*, 5, 933–964.

Riegg Cellini, S., and Goldin, C., 2014, "Does Federal Aid Raise Tuition; New Evidence on For-Profit Colleges," *American Economic Journals: Economic Policy*, 6, 174–206.

Rothwell, J., 2016, "The Declining Productivity of Education," *Social Mobility Memo*, Washington: Brooking Institution.

Silliman, M. and Virtanen, H., 2021, "Labor Market Returns to Vocational Secondary Education," *American Economic Journals: Applied Economics* (forthcoming).

Turner, S., 2004, "Going to College and Finishing College: Explaining Different Educational Outcomes," in *College Decisions: How Students Actually Make Them and How They Could*, C. Hoxby, editor. Chicago: University of Chicago Press.

Ullrich, L., 2021, "Male Labor Force Participation: Patterns and Trends," *Economic Focus* (First Quarter), Richmond Federal Reserve.

Valletta, R., 2018, "The Recent Flattening in the Higher Education Wage Premium: Polarization, Skill Downgrading, or Both?" in Hulten, C. and Ramey, V., editors, *Education, Skills, and Technical Change: Implications for US GDP Growth*, Chicago: University of Chicago Press, pp. 313–342.

Vedder, R., 2019, *Restoring the Promise: Higher education in America*, Oakland: Independent Institute.

Walters, C., 2015, "Inputs in the Production of Early Childhood Education Human Capital: Evidence from Head Start," *American Economic Journal: Applied Economics*, 7, 76–102.

Woessman, L., 2015, "Single-Parent Families and Student Achievement: An International Perspective," Ifo Institute at the University of Munich.

Wu, P., 2022, "Wage Inequality and the Rise in Labor Force Exit: The Case of US Prime-Age Males," *Federal Reserve of Boston Working Papers*, No. 22-16.

Zimmerman, S., 2014, "The Returns to College Admission for Academically Marginal Students," *Journal of Labor Economics*, 32, 711–754.

Zywicki, T., and Koopman, C., 2019, "The Changing of the Guard: The Political Economy of Administrative Bloat in Higher Education," in *Unprofitable Schooling*, Zywicki, T. and McClusky, N. editors, Washington D.C.: Cato Institute.

Chapter 4
International Economic Policy

After WWII, there was a revival and expansion of all types of international economic activity. The current level of international activity has grown to match and even exceed the globalization witnessed in the late nineteenth century and early twentieth century. Globalization is a controversial phenomenon that received strong political opposition during the Trump years when the USA took significant steps toward isolation. How does US international economic activity relate to our twenty-first century challenges and what should be our policy stance toward globalization?

We answer these questions by first assessing the effects on the US economy of all three features of globalization: the trade of goods and services, capital mobility, and immigration. As in previous chapters, our assessment then guides our policy recommendations.

The Trade of Goods and Services

It is important to begin by realizing that, relative to other countries, the USA does not engage in much international trade. US exports of goods and services are between 10% and 15% of GDP. The world's average and the OECD average are twice that amount (World Bank 2023). In addition, US exports of goods have shown remarkably little trend over the *last two centuries*, remaining between 5% and 10% of GDP over the period. US trade in *services* picked up steadily as international activity recovered from WWII, reaching 3–4% of GDP and pushing total US trade into the low teens as a fraction of GDP. In the twenty-first century, US international trade is no longer following the post-WWII upward trend. There has been no upward trend in the US trade of goods and services as a fraction of GDP since 2000. This all means that, despite popular impressions, trading with the rest of the world is not having a major impact, and certainly not a growing impact, on the overall US economy.

© The Author(s), under exclusive license to Springer Nature Switzerland AG 2023

A. Mourmouras, P. Rangazas, *US Economic Policy in the 21st Century*,
Professional Practice in Governance and Public Organizations,
https://doi.org/10.1007/978-3-031-36437-2_4

Effects of Trade on the Average Household

Naturally, there have been attempts to measure the effects of international trade. Textbooks focus on the economy-wide welfare change of making a dramatic move from a perfectly closed to a perfectly open economy. However, finding data on dramatic openings or closings of this type are rare. There is also the issue that when countries change policy toward suddenly opening or closing their economies, they also typically make significant changes in their *domestic* policies as well. For example, in the Asian Tiger "Growth Miracle" countries, there were roughly simultaneous moves to open the economy and to push domestic investment. This makes it difficult to disentangle the separate effects of international trade and domestic policies. Due to these *empirical* difficulties, it is probably true that most economists are primarily convinced of the net benefits of an open economy by the force of the *logical* argument for comparative advantage.

Total Economic Effects from US Trade

Despite the difficulties mentioned above, there is some supporting empirical evidence that opening an economy to international trade creates net welfare benefits. Irwin (2005) estimates the welfare loss to the USA of Jefferson's embargo on trade from 1807 to 1809. In this "natural experiment," Jefferson shut down US international trade for a purely political reason: preventing the harassment of American shipping by the warring British and French navies. The amount of trade, relative to GDP, in 1807 was comparable to that in recent times. US exports were about 13% of GDP. Irwin estimates that the dramatic move to autarky resulted in welfare losses equivalent to a 5% decline in GDP.

The typical approach to estimating the gains from trade, as in Irwin's study, is static in the sense that the resulting rise in real income from changes in relative prices and the reallocation of labor are assumed to have no effect on saving and capital accumulation. As pointed out by Baldwin (1992), the static real income gains will not be entirely consumed, and a portion will be saved and invested in physical capital. Due to capital accumulation, the percentage change in long-run (*steady state*) real income will be a multiple of the initial static increase in real income. Using estimates of the capital share in overall production, the steady-state percentage change in real income will be 1.5 times greater than the initial static percentage change.[1] In the case of the 1807 embargo, the 5% decline in real income would have eventually translated into a 7.5% decline if the embargo had remained in place.

[1] This is based on the effect of trade-based efficiency gains that are equivalent to an increase in total factor productivity (A). An increase in factor productivity raises current real income and eventually steady-state real income ($\overline{y}$) from the resulting saving and capital accumulation. The connection is made via the following formula:

However, the short run-losses made the embargo sufficiently unpopular that it was removed within 2 years.

In the 1980s, economists noticed that the standard model of perfect competition, where trade is based on comparative advantages *across different industries*, was missing something. Much of the trade flows between countries are *within the same industry*. Think of richer countries trading different varieties of automobiles. The model used to address this important observation is one of *monopolistic competition*, where firms produce slightly different brands of the same basic good to carve out a segment of the market and create pricing power. This model of trade not only helped to explain within-industry trade but also revealed new possible gains from trade that are different from the efficiency improvements associated with allocating domestic resources to the most productive industries and importing relatively cheaper products made in less productive industries. There are three newly identified gains of empirical importance from the model of monopolistic competition: an *expansion of product variety* that better meets tastes and raises consumer satisfaction, *reduced monopoly markups* from an increase in foreign competitors, and *productivity improvements within industries* as firms able to compete internationally and expand and those that cannot contract.

The estimation of these gains from trade are based on estimating parameters in models of monopolistic competition that allow a quantitative assessment of how the new gains from trade raise consumer welfare. The first of these quantitative studies focused on product variety alone. As in the approach to quantifying comparative advantage effects, the studies estimate the *change in real income* that yields a welfare gain equivalent to the expanded consumer good variety resulting from trade. Broda and Weinstein (2006) estimate the welfare gain from the expanded variety associated with international trade over the last three decades of the twentieth century was equivalent to a rise in GDP of 2.6%. Feenstra (2010, Ch.2) estimates the total gain from import variety at the end of the twentieth century was equivalent to about 7% of GDP. Ossa (2015) estimated a total gain from trade due to increased variety of both consumer goods and intermediate goods, used in domestic production of final goods, equivalent to a 13.5% increase in GDP.

The product variety studies were expanded to include the gains from foreign competition reducing price markups and from within-industry productivity improvements. Feenstra and Weinstein (2017) find the foreign competition effect was comparable in size to the effect from expanded variety, with the two effects combined generating an estimated welfare gain about the same size as the Broda-Weinstein estimate of the 30-year gain from product variety alone. Feenstra and Kee (2008) estimate that a 3.3% GDP gain over a 20-year period occurred from

---

$$\%\Delta\bar{y} = \frac{1}{1-\alpha} \times \%\Delta A = 1.5 \times \%\Delta A,$$

where α is the capital share of production, estimated to be approximately 1/3. The theory underlining this equation is valid in many different contexts and is reviewed in Ivanyna et al. (2021, pp.133 and 163).

within-industry productivity improvements. Feenstra (2018) estimates all three gains and gets a significantly larger annual gain from trade than the Feenstra and Weinstein (2017) study that focuses only on variety and markup effects.

Thus, there is evidence that the gains from trade exceed those from comparative advantage alone. The gains from the model of monopolistic competition appear to be at least as important. It is not obvious how to combine the estimated gains from studies focused on comparative advantage and those using guidance from models of monopolistic competition. It is likely that the approaches complement each other to a significant degree because they are quite different conceptually. This suggests the *total gains* from US trade could reasonably be equivalent to a gain of GDP in the 10–20% range.

Marginal Effects from Changes in Trade Policy

More common than the attempt to compute the *total* US gains from trade is the attempt to assess the effects of *marginal* changes in trade policy that typically involve increasing or decreasing tariffs. It should be noted that these studies are primarily guided by the simple perfectly competitive model of comparative advantage, so the actual effects could be greater as suggested by the more recent research, summarized above, using the model of monopolistic competition.

An infamous example of a marginal change in policy is the legendary Smoot-Hawley Tariff Act of 1930. In 1930, import tariffs in the USA were raised by 6 percentage points. At the time, US trade was 10% of GDP, somewhat less than it is now. The resulting welfare loss in the USA was equivalent a loss of real income of only about 0.5%.[2] Despite common beliefs to the contrary, the Smoot-Hawley tariff was a very small contributing factor behind the income losses witnessed during the Great Depression.

The North American Free Trade Agreement (NAFTA) of 1994 was a trade agreement between the USA, Canada, and Mexico that lowered tariffs and increased trade flows between the countries. Trade tripled between the USA and the other two countries, who are now the largest destinations for US exports. Before the act was passed, an independent third-party candidate named Ross Perot (a major US auto executive) famously said that if NAFTA passed it would cause "a giant sucking sound of job losses from the US to Mexico." Donald Trump recently called NAFTA the "worst trade deal ever made." He pushed for a renegotiation to make it a better trade deal for the USA but those efforts led to very minor changes.

Contrary to the dramatic claims from politicians, economists agree that all three countries benefited from NAFTA. There was a net loss of about 15,000 jobs in the USA but there were gains in the average real wage because the new jobs created were associated with higher worker productivity than the jobs lost and because of the

[2] Bond et al. (2013) and Mitchener et al. (2021).

lower relative prices of imports that raised consumer purchasing power. For every job lost, there was a gain in real income of $450,000. The overall effect was equivalent to a rise in real income of about 0.5%.[3]

More recently, we saw the Trump tariffs in 2018. Trump increased tariffs between 10% and 50% across a variety of imports from different countries, with a special focus on Chinese imports. Estimates indicate the overall effect was a deadweight loss to the US economy of $7–$8 billion in 2018, less than 0.5% of GDP.[4]

The Welfare Effects of US Trade: Summary

There is powerful logic and supporting empirical evidence that countries generally benefit from international trade. Naturally, the more involved a country is in trade, the larger the benefits. The USA is a large and diversified economy that does not trade as much, as a fraction of GDP, as most countries. The *total* net benefits from international trade by the USA are still significant, somewhere between 10% and 20% of GDP. *Marginal* changes in trade associated with tariff increases and decreases, such as those we have witnessed over our history since the early twentieth century, have relatively small net effects, less than 1% of GDP. The USA should be careful not to make large departures from free trade but even its most notable changes in tariffs have had relatively small effects on the economy. While the net effects on the economy of marginal changes in tariff policies are minor, there could be more substantial effects felt by particular groups. Our next section looks at the *distributional* effects of trade.

Distributional Effects from Trade

International trade benefits an economy on average but also creates winners and losers within the economy. Trade causes some industries and regions of a country to expand while causing others to contract. The expansion of international trade since the 1970s occurred at the same time that wage and income inequality rose.[5] In 1980, the wages of college graduates were about 40% higher than high school graduates. By 2000, college graduates made almost double the wage of high school graduates. Was this *correlation* largely a coincidence or was trade a key factor *causing* inequality to increase?

---

[3] Chatzky et al. (2020).

[4] Amiti et al. (2019) and Fajgelbaum et al. (2020). For a recent survey of the research on the Trump tariffs, see Fajgelbaum and Khandelwal (2022). The common conclusion is that the US consumer paid for the brunt of the tariffs but that the total welfare loss for the USA was small.

[5] Helpman (2018) provides an authoritative survey of the effects of trade on inequality.

Standard Argument for a Link Between Trade and Inequality

Some of the expansion in US trade since the 1970s is with less developed economies such as Mexico and China. These countries began exporting many goods into the USA that were produced primarily with low-skilled labor. For example, Mexico exports machinery, mechanical parts, and agricultural products, while China exports electronics, metals, and textiles. The theory of comparative advantage predicts trade lowers the relative price of imported products, causing domestic production of these goods to contract. The contraction of industries that employ low-skilled labor causes a reduction in low-skilled wages. In addition, trade has increased the international demand and relative price of goods that we export which includes many goods from industries that employ primarily high-skilled labor such as financial services, commercial airplanes, and high-tech equipment. Theory suggests the expansion of these export industries increase the demand and wages of high-skilled workers.

Contrary to these sensible predictions, the empirical evidence indicates that US trade has caused little or no effect on the relative price of high-skilled intensive sectors or on the relative wage of skilled labor. This was a consistent finding from a variety of studies including those by Katz and Murphy (1992), Borjas et al. (1997), Leamer (1998), and Freenstra (2015). It turns out that the USA also has comparative advantages in sectors that use low-skilled labor such as agriculture and automobiles. Natural resources, technologies, product variety, and not only the abundance of high-skilled labor create comparative advantages in US industries. The relative abundance of skilled labor in the USA is not a dominant factor in explaining our trade patterns with developing countries and thus the predictions based on this source of comparative advantage alone have not materialized.

Other Ways Trade May Raise Inequality

It does not appear that comparative advantage created trade patterns that worsened inequality in the USA. Nevertheless, the correlation between rising trade and rising inequality has encouraged economists to look for more subtle mechanisms through which trade may cause greater income inequality.

Many technological innovations in recent decades have been related to the emergence of the computer as an important capital input to the production of goods and services. It is also true that college-educated workers use the computer on the job much more than those with less than a college education. In 1984 the share of hours worked with a computer was 45.5% for workers with a college degree and 22.1% for workers with less than a college degree. In 2003, these numbers were 85.7% and 45.3%, respectively. The computer is a highly complementary productive input for high-skilled labor. Perhaps international trade has lowered the relative price of computers in the USA, which would advantage skilled labor relative to unskilled labor.

Burstein et al. (2019) look at this possibility and find very small effects. International trade lowered the relative price of computers so slightly that it could only explain a small rise in computer use at the workplace. As a result, the use of the computer, due to *international trade* affecting its relative price, only raised the premium paid to college-educated workers by 2 percentage points of the total 50 percentage point rise in the college wage premium mentioned above.

Another mechanism linking trade to inequality considers the possibility that industries facing import competition may be concentrated in some regions of the country while exporters may be concentrated in others. If workers are imperfectly mobile across regions, then expanded trade could raise the wage dispersion across the country and increase wage inequality. Caliendo et al. (2019) look at the regional effects of our trade surge with China. They find the trade surge caused a small positive effect on employment overall with a reduction in manufacturing employment but a somewhat larger increase in services, retail trade, and construction. However, the decline in manufacturing was regionally concentrated in states such as California and Texas where wages also fell. While trade has not affected the relative position of high- and low-skilled workers nationally, it has led to some wage dispersion *within* skill classes *across regions*.

This research has been confirmed in other studies. For example, Bloom et al. (2019) find a reallocation of US jobs from manufacturing to services caused by trade with China. The loss in manufacturing jobs was concentrated in low human capital areas (South and Mid-West) and the gains in service jobs were concentrated in high human capital areas (West and East coasts). However, there was no evidence of worker regional migration due to these structural changes, suggesting different regional effects from trade on workers' wages as found by Caliendo et al. (2019). Given that the job reallocation before 2007 was from low human capital to high human capital regions, there may have been a rise in the college premium as well. There was no evidence of a net loss in jobs nationally and no employment effects of any type after 2007. It is interesting that some of the job re-allocation took place within the same large companies that shifted their focus from less domestic production to greater research, design, management, and marketing. Examples include Apple, Techtronic Industries (e.g., including Milwaukee Electric Tool and Hoover), and Bernhardt Furniture.

Residual inequality is wage inequality *within a skill group*, e.g., wage dispersion *among* college educated workers. The increase in the overall inequality we have seen this century is largely due to higher residual inequality among college graduates. The *regional disparity* in wages caused by trade with China is one possible explanation for residual inequality. Another reason for differential pay received by workers at similar skill levels is the *wage-size premium*—workers in larger firms make more than their counterparts working in smaller firms. One reason for this, for example, could be that larger firms do more on-the-job training of their employees that raises their skill level in tasks the firm requires them to do. Exporting firms in the USA are larger than firms that face import competition. Thus, expanded trade could make the size gap between exporting and importing firms even greater, thereby increasing residual inequality. This is an interesting possible explanation for increased residual inequality but there is no empirical study that confirms its importance. There are also other competing explanations for the rise in residual inequality based on the increased importance of the *major* of a college graduate and whether the college graduate goes on to receive a *higher-level degree*, as we reviewed in Chap. 3.

Distributional Effects of Trade: Summary

While the rise in wage inequality is correlated with the rise in international trade over the last 40 years, this is primarily a coincidence. Trade has not been an important causal factor in driving inequality higher. Important causes of the rise in inequality are skill-biased technological change related to the expanded use of the computer at the workplace and an excess demand for college-educated workers, especially for STEM majors and those go on to receive graduate degrees. The only significant effect that trade appears to have on the dispersion of wages is based on regional disparities in the concentration of exporting industries and industries facing import competition.

International Trade of Assets

Assets, and not just goods, are traded across borders. When assets can be traded across borders, capital is said to be *mobile*. The trade of assets is what creates the possibility that the trade of goods might not balance, i.e., why a country might run a *trade deficit* or *surplus* where exports fall short of or exceed imports. Understanding the link between asset trading and goods trading helps assess the economic effects of the persistent US trade deficit, a topic of emphasis in trade policy discussion.

Foreign investment consists of *portfolio investment* (new purchases of foreign financial assets such as stocks and bonds) and *direct investment* (new purchases of physical capital in a foreign country to set up a multinational business). A country's ownership of foreign assets net of its foreign liabilities (foreigners' holdings of its assets) is called its *net foreign investment position*. This is a misleading name because investment is a flow term that should refer to the *change* in assets not the *stock* of assets currently owned. A better name would be net foreign asset position. Foreign investment is the increase or decrease in the country's net foreign asset position that occurs over time.

Now for a little accounting that links the trade of goods and the trade of assets. The trade of assets creates a potential source of income, the return earned on the country's net holding of foreign assets (which can be negative if a country holds net liabilities). This creates a difference between GNP (income flowing to a country's citizens or nationals) and GDP (income created within a country's domestic borders). GNP is GDP plus the return earned from net holding of foreign assets.

GNP is used to either purchase goods and services (no matter where they are produced) or to buy new foreign assets (carry out net foreign investment), so GDP + the return earned from net holding of foreign assets = goods and service purchases + net foreign investment. If one subtracts purchases from both sides of the equality, you get *net exports* (GDP minus the purchases of goods and services) + the return from net foreign assets = net foreign investment. Accounting alone establishes that net exports are tightly linked to net foreign investment.

Countries running *trade deficits* are likely carrying out negative foreign investment—i.e., accumulating foreign liabilities or *borrowing* from foreign countries.

Countries running *trade surpluses* are likely carrying out positive foreign investment—i.e., accumulating foreign assets or *lending* to foreign countries.

If we can understand why a country is an international borrower or lender, then we can understand why it is running a trade deficit or surplus on the goods account.

Foreign investment occurs when there is a difference between what a country saves, called *national saving*, and its *domestic investment*. Trade deficits occur when a country's national saving is low relative to its domestic investment opportunities. If foreigners are willing to fund the gap between the home country's domestic investment and its national saving, this necessarily means that foreigners are using currency earned from selling their exports to buy assets, not goods, from the home country.

Thus, a trade deficit implies a country is experiencing insufficient national saving to cover its domestic investment opportunities. This scenario suggests that without foreign funding, the country would not experience as much investment and thus would grow more slowly. Slower growth in physical capital and domestic production also means slower growth in wages. So, in terms of long-run growth and household welfare in the future, a trade deficit is clearly not bad.

We can look at this claim in more detail by considering the two times in US history when the country ran persistent trade deficits. In both cases, the USA experienced a shortfall of national saving needed to fund domestic investment. However, in one case it was because of unusually high investment and in the other case it was because of unusually low national saving.

1800–1880 The US Industrial Revolution

The UK and Europe began experiencing an industrial revolution that created sustained economic growth for the first time in human history around 1800, shortly before or shortly after, depending on the country. The major offshoots of the UK (Canada, Australia, New Zealand, and the USA) began their industrial revolution a bit later.

The industrial revolution was created by important technological progress that greatly enhanced the use of man-made physical capital in the production of goods—

factories, public infrastructure such as railroads, and new types of farm equipment. The technological advances expanded profitable investment opportunities that were greater than those one could make from land purchases, the main investment activity in earlier history.

When these technological innovations were brought to the USA, there was not sufficient national saving to fund the related investments because the USA was still a middle-income country. Richer countries in Europe, particularly England, had the saving to fund these new investments that were yielding relatively high returns in the USA. When England exported goods to the USA, the proceeds were used to fund investments by purchasing US assets instead of US goods and a US trade deficit resulted. This was clearly good for the USA because the economic growth over this period would not have been as fast without the funding from England. When a trade deficit results from technological progress that increases investment demand, it is hard to find fault in the situation.

1980–Present

For several reasons, the US national saving rate has trended downward over the last 40 years (see Chaps. 1 and 2). Domestic investment has also declined but not as sharply, creating a gap between investment and national saving. The US return on investment has remained high relative to that in other advanced countries. As a result, foreign saving from around the world has filled the financing gap leading to a persistent trade deficit for the USA.

The scenario of a trade deficit caused by increasing consumption and declining national saving is not as unambiguously positive as trade deficits caused by booming domestic investment opportunities. Nevertheless, the decline in national saving would have caused a larger decline in US domestic investment and slower growth if it were not for the rise in foreign financing. Domestic US policy, and not trade policy, has contributed to the decline in national saving. The trade deficit reflects inflows of foreign saving that have mediated the negative effects of low national saving on capital accumulation and economic growth.

Problematic Persistent Trade Deficits?

Fundamentally there is no economic harm from trade deficits; quite the contrary, they help a country grow faster. However, there may be political concerns with trade imbalances that eventually create economic problems.

First, given the general misunderstanding of trade imbalances, it can cause the public and politicians to blame trade for the country's economic problems. This leads to protectionist policies that lower trade and average welfare in the trading countries. For example, there is no doubt that the Trump tariffs were, at least partially, motivated by our persistent trade deficit.

Second, a trade imbalance can reflect an over-reliance on either foreign demand for goods, in the case of countries running persistent trade surpluses, or foreign capital inflows, in the case of countries running persistent trade deficits. This means the country with large trade imbalances depend on foreign behavior that is largely out of their control and that could abruptly change beyond the influence of its own domestic policy. The dependence is particularly problematic when the two countries are political adversaries, like the USA and China.

The way to address large and persistent trade deficits is with *domestic fiscal policy* that increases national saving to bring it more in line with domestic investment opportunities. The policy recommendations to deal with the US fiscal crisis in Chap. 2 will reduce the US trade deficit for economically and politically sound reasons.

Offshoring

Our capital mobility discussion included *foreign direct investment*, where foreign companies set up shop in different countries and produce a final product that is sold to domestic markets. However, foreign direct investment has combined with the fragmentation of production to create a more complex picture.

The *fragmentation* or *unbundling* of the production process means that the design, production, assembly, marketing, and servicing of a single final product involves distinct tasks that may take place in different locations. When some tasks take place in a different country, they are said to be *offshored*. This creates the global supply chains that were prominent in the news during the pandemic. The offshored production could take place in a factory of a foreign business partner or a multinational branch of a domestic firm. Offshoring means there can be flows of exports and imports even within the same company. Two-thirds of global trade is now made up of intermediate inputs rather than final goods consumed by households.

iPhones enter the USA as imports from China. The assembly involves a product design that originates in the USA and many component parts from all over the world. Ford engines are produced in Ford plants in Mexico and enter the USA as imports but then are exported out as part of a truck. When we levy tariffs on imported iPhones and Ford engines, we are taxing not only US consumers but also US companies and not just foreign ones.

Technological advancements have lowered transportation and communication costs, contributing to fragmentation. Since the 1990s, there has been a rise in the ratio of *final good export value* to the *value added* in the production process by the country exporting the good. For example, when this ratio has a value of 2 it means that the final good is twice as valuable as the value contributed to the product by the exporting country. This happens because much of the value of the final product was not created in the exporting country but instead was first produced and imported into the exporting country.

What are the effects of product fragmentation and offshoring of production tasks on the real wages and welfare of US households? As with our other international activities, there is concern that offshoring drives down wages of low-skilled workers. US companies offshore tasks, such as the assembly of iPhones, that could be done by low-skilled labor in the USA. As with trade of final goods, the common misperception is that offshoring is done because low-skilled labor in the foreign country is cheaper. However, if lower pay reflects lower productivity in the tasks being offshored, then the company would not get ahead by shifting that production task abroad. Thus, offshoring of production occurs when our low-skilled labor has productivity in the offshored tasks that is lower than in other domestic uses, while foreign low-skilled labor has productivity in those tasks that is higher than in other production in their country. The same comparative advantage logic applies to offshoring as to the trade of final goods—produce the component where the *relative* productivity *within* a country is highest and the relative price is lowest.

The question is whether the job loss associated with the offshored tasks can be offset by greater employment in jobs where low-skilled US labor is more productive, just as when comparative advantage logic is applied to final goods. More productive job opportunities may increase because the offshoring makes US firms more profitable, causing firms' total output to expand. Thus, offshoring could benefit US low-skilled labor by shifting them to tasks where they are relatively more productive, either within the companies offshoring or elsewhere in the economy. An increase in the productivity of labor implies an increase in the real wage.

A study by Wright (2014) examined the empirical strength of two effects, related to the discussion above, associated with offshoring of production tasks to China. The results reported are scaled to a one percentage point rise in offshoring to China between 2001 and 2007. The *direct effect* was a *decline* in low-skilled manufacturing labor hours by *228,000* due to offshored production tasks (about one fifth of 1.2 million decline in US low-skilled manufacturing hours over the period). The *indirect effect* was to *expand production by 1%* resulting in about 70% of the low-skilled workers initially laid off to be *rehired to do other production tasks*, a gain in employment of *159,600* labor hours. The net effect was 68,400 labor hours lost, about *6% of the total loss in manufacturing hours* between 2001 and 2007. So, offshoring to China had a small negative effect on employment and was certainly not the main reason for the decline in US manufacturing employment. Unfortunately, the study did not estimate wage effects. These would likely be smaller negative values, or perhaps even positive, if the low-skilled US labor was generally shifted to higher productivity tasks.

The China case study establishes that there can be small negative effects on employment of low-skilled US labor due to offshoring. The negative employment effects presumably would limit, at least to some degree, any positive wage effects from increasing low-skilled productivity (by the shift to higher productivity tasks). The negative employment concern does not arise for high-skilled labor. The expanded firm production from the cost saving of offshoring would only raise the demand for high-skilled workers and thus increase their wages. These considerations suggest that offshoring could increase wage inequality (even if the wages of low-skilled workers rise somewhat, the wages of high skilled labor are likely to rise more).

A second study, by Feenstra and Hanson (1999), addresses the effect of offshoring on wage inequality. It covers the decade of the 1980s, a period of increased US FDI. For example, there was an expansion in US FDI in Mexico during the 1980s that expanded the share of imported intermediate goods used in US manufacturing, consistent with the rise in the intermediate good share in world trade generally.

The authors estimated the effect of this offshoring on the rise in the US college premium from 1979 to 1990 (a period where the premium rose a lot, see Chap. 3). Their estimates suggest about 1/5 of the increase in the college premium can be explained by offshoring. The remainder of the rise in wage inequality is explained by a rise in the use of high-tech equipment in manufacturing firms. This matches the general conclusion that international activity has had some effect on greater wage inequality but is not the main driver.

Offshoring and global supply chains are on the rise due to increased mobility of physical capital and technology. It appears that this is at least a minor reason for the rise in wage inequality in the USA due to a contraction in manufacturing jobs. There are two other policy issues associated with offshoring. First, foreign direct investment makes property rights over technology a major issue in trade agreements. Offshoring that involves foreign partners would seem to make it even harder to maintain rights over production ideas. Second, given the mobility of physical capital and technology, investment in human capital, the least mobile of production inputs, is the best way to raise a *nation's* wealth and attract foreign investment. In particular, investment in middle-level skills can be used in producing services that cannot be easily offshored. Labor with middle-skills are needed in high-tech and transportation equipment maintenance and repair, health services, plumbing, and construction, to name a few. Investment in middle-skills reduces offshoring, raises investment in the USA and wages, and reduces wage inequality. This consideration offers another justification for shifting US investments toward vocational training as argued in Chap. 3.

Immigration

The inflow of foreign people into the USA is as contentious as the international trade of goods and assets. As with trade, immigration is not as large as many people imagine. The share of foreign-born people in the US population has risen slowly since the mid-twentieth century to reach about 13%. This is a bit less than in the nineteenth-century USA and close to the shares in European countries today. The US immigrant share is much lower than the 25% share found in Canada and in Australia.

Since 2000, the US immigrant share has grown slower than in other rich countries. As we shall see, this is a cause of concern for the US economy because immigration can help restore faster growth and solve the fiscal crisis.[6]

Economic Effects of Immigration

The standard thinking about the economic effects of immigration is that immigration increases the supply of labor and lowers wages. This view can be defended using a model where all *workers are substitutes* for one another (i.e., all do the same production tasks with some doing them better than others) and where the *physical capital stock and the production technology are fixed* (the number and size of firms are fixed, as are the ideas about products and production methods). Under these assumptions, an increase in the *supply* of labor lowers the marginal productivity of labor and wages must fall to encourage firms to increase employment.[7]

The conclusion of the standard view is that immigration lowers living standards for native workers by lowering their wages. Thus, the cultural objections over immigration that some natives hold are supported by a potentially important economic objection. The problem with the economics of the standard view is that it ignores several reasons why the *demand* for labor may increase as a result of immigration. If the demand for labor were to increase, then wages would not necessarily fall to clear the labor market. There are several reasons why immigration may increase labor demand that are missed in the basic model supporting the standard view.

Physical Capital Adjustment

In the standard view, the capital-labor ratio falls with immigration, causing a decline in the marginal productivity of labor that leads to lower wages. The decline in the capital-labor ratio is due to the assumption that the capital stock is fixed. However, the capital stock will also rise with immigration. Immigrants save a portion of their wages just as native workers do. Through financial intermediaries, the increase in saving provides additional funding for firms' investment projects that increase the economy's physical capital stock. The increase in the number and size of firms increases the demand for labor and pushes wages back up.

---

[6]Most of the background material we use in this section comes from the survey of the immigration literature by Peri (2016).

[7]The Appendix gives a formal description of the model supporting the standard view and the more nuanced models that challenge it. The model is also useful for understanding the effect of skill-biased technological progress on wage inequality.

In an economy that is open to international capital movement, the increase in the capital stock would happen even faster. The increase in the supply of labor, while lowering the marginal product of labor, raises the marginal product of capital and the return to capital owners. The higher returns attract companies and lenders around the world to invest in the USA until the wages for workers and the returns to investment are back in line with their pre-immigration levels.

If immigration is concentrated in particular locations within a country, the capital adjustments will occur by companies moving toward areas where wages and labor costs are low. These adjustments in capital location will continue until the wages in the areas most affected by immigration are similar to those elsewhere in the country.

Heterogeneous Labor and Complementarity of Inputs

Another problem with the standard approach is the assumption that all workers are perfect *substitutes*. It is more likely that workers at different skill levels or who perform different production tasks are *complements* in production. For example, managers and factory workers, manual and customer service workers, and quantitative analysts and marketing agents are pairs of employment types that play different roles and that enhance one another's productivity.

The complementarity of different types of labor is particularly relevant in understanding the effect of US immigration because immigration here is concentrated at the extreme ends of the education distribution. US immigrants make up 40% of high school dropouts and 30% of PhDs. If these two groups are complements in production, then the effects of overall immigration are quite different than under the perfect substitutes assumption. More specifically, wages of the workers at the two extremes of the education distribution are a function of the *shares* of the two types of workers in total employment (see Appendix). If immigration does not change the mix of these shares, then the wages of both types will be unaffected.

Externalities and Technological Progress

There is evidence suggesting that immigrants contribute disproportionately to the creation of new products and new business formation. In contrast, the standard approach assumes there is no effect of immigration on production technology. The US immigration share is only 13% of the total workforce but this group contributes 25% of US global patents and 30% of new business formation.[8] New business formation and technological progress raise wages, helping to offset any negative wage effects from an increase in the supply of labor.

---

[8]Wadhwa (2012).

Empirical Evidence

Empirical studies at the *national* level find very little effect of immigration on the average wages of both skilled and unskilled labor. This is, in part, due to the balanced effect of US immigration on the shares of skilled and unskilled labor in the workforce. This could change if immigration patterns change and cause changes in the relative mix of worker types. Another reason for the lack of a national impact on US wages is that the gradual increase in immigration over the last 50 years has allowed the capital stock to increase and keep the national capital-labor ratio relatively constant.

While in the country overall wages are not much impacted by immigration, this may not be the case in locations where immigration, especially of low-skilled types, are most concentrated. However, careful studies of immigrant inflows to particular locations, due either to the presence of a supportive ethnic community or due to dramatic political events that cause sudden changes in the immigrant population, do not find that immigration lowers low-skilled wages. This is partly due to the contribution of low-skilled immigrants to new business formation. There is also some evidence that native low-skilled workers shift toward service work (due to their advantage in language skills), leaving manual work for the immigrant population. This is a type of complementary *within* the category of low-skilled labor that works in a similar way as the complementary between low- and high-skilled labor.

Studies of immigration of high-skilled labor find positive effects on the US economy. H-1B visas are temporary work visas for jobs requiring a college degree. These types of visas are capped but the cap is raised or lowered in given years. These cap variations identify temporary shifts in the supply of skilled labor coming into the USA. The shifts in the supply of skilled labor from cap variations are estimated to be positively correlated with US patents and the wages of skilled labor across the country. This suggests that an influx of skilled labor from outside the USA increases productivity of native high-skilled types via technology improvements more than it causes marginal productivity to fall via increases in the share of high-skilled labor in the workforce.

Studies of the effects of immigrants entering US higher education are consistent with the technology story. Immigrants entering US higher education raise technological know-how. This could happen due to university research or the applied research and development they do in the USA after graduation. Hunt and Gauthier-Loiselle (2010) estimate that a 1 percentage point increase in the immigration share of US college graduates increases patents per capita by 9–18%. Their estimates suggest that over the 1990s, the 1.3 percentage point increase in the immigrant share of college graduates raised patenting between 12% and 21%. Bilgin et al. (2021) find a country's foreign student share has a robust positive association with economic growth in a cross-section of OECD countries, even in the presence of many control variables that account for the possible reverse causation from growth to foreign student enrollment.

Summary

There is little or no evidence for the basic-model prediction that immigration lowers the wages of native workers at *any* skill level. In the USA, this is in part because of a relatively balanced mix of skilled and unskilled workers that are complementary inputs in production. However, even when immigration is not balanced, there are other forces that keep wages from falling or even cause rising wages over time. These forces include the formation of physical capital, especially in sectors and locations where the immigrants are concentrated, and, in the case of skilled immigration, the creation of new production technology that raises overall economic growth.

The general population largely recognizes the economic benefits of US immigration. A 2021 Gallup poll found that 75% of Americans considered immigration to be good for the USA. Even when asked about illegal immigrants, a 2019 survey by the Pew Research Center found that 67% of Americans favor finding a way for illegals to remain in the USA legally. However, attitudes about immigration generally can be poisoned by border crises where the government loses control of entry into the country.

Border Crises

The same polls mentioned above indicate that the majority of Americans believe that illegal immigration is a problem because of safety and security concerns. During normal times, immigration is a fairly orderly and planned process driven by wage differentials across countries. However, controlling immigration becomes difficult when there are dramatic increases in immigrants who are refugees and asylum seekers from wars and oppressive political regimes. Despite the fact that most people want to take in refugees and asylum seekers (73% in the Pew 2019 survey), they are uncomfortable with a loss of control at the border. Pressures at the borders will only increase as climate change causes migration from developing countries that experience natural disasters and deteriorating economic conditions.

In recent years, desperate border situations confront Europe because of the Russia-Ukraine conflict and the USA because of failed regimes in countries such as Venezuela, Cuba, and Nicaragua. For example, prior to 2013 almost all of those crossing the USA-Mexico border were Mexican citizens seeking better employment opportunities. Since then, the majority of those crossing the USA-Mexico border first entered Mexico from Central America, reaching 81% of US immigrants from Mexico by 2019 (Klobucista et al. 2022). In the future, climate change also has the potential to create natural disasters that will cause dramatic and sudden increases in immigration flows into the USA and other rich countries with colder climates.

In these desperate situations, relying solely on border security does not work (it is not clear that this point is recognized by the public). Over the past decade, the USA has spent more on border security while the borders have become less secure. The harder it is for desperate people to cross a border, the more they will turn to criminal cartels to assist their journey, worsening illegal immigration and the organized crime associated with it (Alden 2022). A more sensible approach starts with international cooperation to share the burden of sudden immigrant inflows and expediated asylum processing, including denials to some that do not merit special consideration, to keep the legal channels open.

In addition, destination governments should realize that refugee inflows represent both a challenge and an opportunity. Common sense suggests and research confirms that refugees as a group have a more difficult time assimilating into host country labor markets than do immigrants motivated by purely economic considerations, who are often assisted by family connections. However, countries with labor shortages, as in the USA, could benefit from refugee inflows in the long run if the proper short-run investments are made. Recent studies show that an exposure to language training and placement of immigrants in strong labor markets could raise earnings of immigration well above the investment costs. For example, in a study based on data from Denmark, a 3-year language program has a present value cost of $2762 per refugee. The present value of additional earnings to the immigrant, over a 15-year period, due to the program was $30,045 (Foged et al. 2022). Greater investments in processing and assimilating deserving immigrants can pay long-run dividends for the USA as well.

Policy Suggestions to Benefit More from International Activity

The USA has gained from international trade, and it should avoid any significant backsliding toward isolationism. With recent events pushing the world toward a new Cold War, the USA should focus on trading more with its allies, but not completely cutoff trade with Russia and China. Economic interdependence reduces the chance of direct conflict and increases the likelihood of needed cooperation on climate change policy (see Chapter 5).

The best way to foster beneficial trade generally is to improve our *domestic* policy, following the suggestions in the chapters on fiscal policy and human capital policy. Taking steps to avoid a fiscal crisis will bring our national saving more in line with our domestic investment. This will reduce our excessive dependence on foreign saving and reduce our trade deficit. Smaller trade deficits decrease the chance of misguided moves toward protectionism that would lower the average welfare of US households. Providing workers with productive skills through a reformed education system and improved overall public infrastructure will allow more households to gain from international capital flows.

Evidence suggests that both the expansion of trade with China and the rise in offshoring have contributed to, although in a relatively minor way, US income inequality. Greater investment in public infrastructure and a more efficient allocation of human capital investment in worker skills will increase the return to physical capital and raise labor productivity across all production tasks and worker skill levels. This makes the USA a more attractive place for multinational companies to do business and will reduce offshoring by US companies.

The major causes of rising inequality are skill-biased technological progress and an outdated education strategy that attempts to send all workers to college, where the education standards are slipping. Empirical evidence suggests there is little effect of immigration on wage inequality. The Appendix contains a production model that can be used to articulate how unskilled labor, skilled labor, and machines relate to each other in the production process. The main purpose of the model is to discuss one of the reasons why a balanced immigration policy does not impact wage inequality. The last portion of the Appendix uses the model to explain the important effect of skill-biased technological change on wage inequality.

Restrictive immigration policy will not reduce wage inequality in the USA. Wage inequality should be addressed with reforms to domestic education policy. As discussed in Chap. 3, public education dollars should be reallocated to high return investments in preschool education and vocational training in high school and away from the disproportionate and inefficient support for higher education. A reallocation of human capital investment gives all children the early investments that will ensure a solid base in literacy and numeracy needed to be productive adults. Rather than favoring college-prep training for high school students, many students would prefer and benefit more from vocational skills to help them *work with* new technology and machines, rather than be *replaced by* these innovations. Fighting the fundamental domestic sources of inequality also allows the USA to get the most out of globalization by attracting foreign firms and by reducing offshoring of middle-skill production tasks.

Aging, a stylized fact associated with the late stages of economic development, is a reason the USA and other advanced economies need greater immigration across *all* skill levels. A major reason for the fiscal crisis is the aging of the US population and a decline in the worker–to-retiree ratio. US immigrants tend to be younger and many are highly educated. The average lifetime contribution to net taxes (taxes minus transfers) of a US immigrant in the last 10 years is over $170,000 (Peri 2022).

There is no economic basis for reducing legal US immigration. Immigration will increase the population share of younger tax-paying workers needed to finance the care of the growing population of retired households, easing the fiscal crisis. Attracting high-skilled immigration from around the world makes it more likely that the USA will remain a major source of technological innovation. Teamed with workers possessing improved vocational skills from the needed domestic education reforms, the spillovers of these innovations are more likely to stay home and raise economic growth and the standard of living throughout the population.

As a practical example, the policy principles just outlined can be applied to assess the new CHIPS and Science Act (Krueger 2022). The Act provides $50 billion in government support to strengthen the domestic semiconductor industry with the goal of making the USA a more self-sufficient country. About 20% of the funds will be allocated to research and development, with 80% going to subsidize private factory investment. This breakdown of the Act's budget indicates a misallocation of public funds. The government should raise productivity by funding basic research and public infrastructure that *generally* supports private investment in the USA, rather than directing the allocation of private investment across industries. Industrial policy that channels public funds to particular investment projects is risky, especially in the case of plants making semiconductors.

The technology of semiconductors continues to evolve rapidly. The state-of-the-art versions of semiconductors require different production equipment from past vintages. Government-guided investment in physical plant and equipment could easily be obsolete in a few years. In addition, the USA currently lacks key labor market skills needed to operate these plants—for example, electrical engineers, software developers, print technicians, and production line specialists. The US skill deficiency in the semiconductor industry is another example of why we need a combination of improved vocational education to build middle-skills and easier immigration for students and labor with higher level skills.

The Taiwan Semiconductor Manufacturing Company (TSMC) opened a chip plant on December 6 2022 in Arizona, an event that should exemplify how the USA is benefiting from globalization (Ting-Fang 2022). The founding father of TSMC, Morris Chang, tempered the excitement over opening the new plant by commenting that geopolitics have drastically changed the situation facing semiconductor makers and warned that "globalization and free trade are almost dead." It is a fine goal for the USA to seek some domestic production for semiconductor chips but an efficient and resilient supply chain structure needs open competition and diversification.

The best way for the USA to gain from developments in the semiconductor industry, and any other industry, is to rely on an open economy environment where our ability to compete for multinationals is enhanced by government support for basic research and public infrastructure, weaker immigration restrictions, and a reallocation of education spending to develop middle-skills.

Foreign Aid

The USA tries to promote economic development across the globe. Economic development reduces conflict, promotes stability, and creates trade relationships, all benefiting the USA. Foreign aid, when successful, is also an important tool in controlling large migration flows out of countries with poor economic conditions. As we discuss in Chap. 5, development is important for a country's ability to cope and adjust to climate change, another important factor in controlling future migration flows. US economic aid is a crucial part of its overall policy strategy.

Unfortunately, it is a discouraging stylized fact about development that no robust correlation between aid and growth has been identified in the econometric literature (e.g., Easterly et al. 2004). There are several possible econometric reasons for the absence of a clear positive relationship, for example, *endogeneity of aid flows* (aid is targeted to slow-growing economies), *specification error* (the relationship between aid and growth is highly nonlinear), and *measurement error* (all aid, including aid not intended to generate growth, is lumped together in a single measure). Attempts to account for these econometric issues have failed to overturn the consensus finding of a zero correlation between aid and growth (see, e.g., Rajan and Subramanian 2008, 2011).

Das et al. (2018, Ch.5) use a calibrated growth model to highlight some of the fundamental reasons that aid might not work. They start by identifying two quantitatively important reasons that a developing country fails to converge toward the economic prosperity of richer countries. One is a *poverty trap* that keeps schooling low and fertility high. The second is a *fiscal policy* chosen by a government that attaches a low value to the future welfare of the country's private sector households. The fiscal policy that maximizes the welfare of public officials is characterized by high tax rates, high government consumption, and low government infrastructure investment. These two fundamentals are shown to create large labor productivity gaps between rich and poor countries that do not dissipate over time. The model is then used to evaluate the effects of aid and policy reforms designed to promote growth. Below is summary of the lessons learned from the analysis.

Unconditional Aid Is Not Growth-Promoting

Unconditional aid is where resources are provided to supplement the government budgets of developing countries with no strings attached on how the resources are used. The simulation results suggest that unconditional aid, including aid where conditions are not adequately enforced, will not deliver any long-term gains in income. The boost to growth from unconditional aid is short-lived and so modest that it could easily be overshadowed by other developments—e.g., any long-lasting effects of the negative shocks to the economy that initially triggered the scaling up of unconditional aid to begin with.

Domestic Conflict over Growth Policies

While there are policies that can generate rapid growth and sustained increases in income, there is likely to be domestic conflict over which policy to pursue. The government favors opening the economy and compulsory schooling, but the current generation of private households will oppose both policies. The current generation of private households favors a program that uses subsidies to replace the forgone wages of older children when they attend school. On costs grounds, the government views the subsidy program as clearly inferior to compulsory schooling. Household opposition to imposed compulsory schooling makes enforcement of the policy difficult. These conflicts may undermine attempts to achieve domestic consensus over which growth-promoting and poverty-reducing policies to implement. Such lack of consensus could delay or undermine the negotiation and implementation of conditional aid agreements with donors.

Prohibitive Aid Cost

Fiscal reforms are often part of the conditions for receiving aid. Simulations using the growth model suggest that reforms of domestic fiscal policy are likely to be the least successful of the policies that examined. First, the growth effects of fiscal reform are relatively modest and short-lived. Second, the aid-cost of "buying" the reforms from the poor country's government are enormous. Unless the aid keeps flowing to the poor country in sufficient quantity, the domestic government will do what it can to revert back to a high-tax, low-investment regime. In fact, the cost of maintaining effective reforms will increase over time as the government's budget, and the potential to increase government consumption, grows. In practice, aid is likely to be far less than what is necessary to keep the government indifferent and thus fiscal reforms may be doomed from the beginning.

Even if the aid is carried out in sufficient amounts indefinitely, there will be little correlation between aid and economic growth in the data. The growth effects occur early on, while the aid continues in the future, during periods where the growth effects have long since vanished. If aid is reduced or maintained at constant level, rather than increased, there will be a reversion in fiscal policy and growth. Thus, aid could be flowing to a country experiencing negative growth.

Humanitarian Aid

The growth model analysis reveals that there can be significant difficulties associated with using foreign aid to finance large-scale government investment projects or to induce changes in national policy. When the confidence in the foreign government is low, it is natural to think of bypassing the government in the seemingly less ambitious goal of providing humanitarian aid directly to the country's poor. Unfortunately, even providing food to the poor people of a country is difficult.

Nunn and Qian (2014) summarize the problems with providing humanitarian aid. Food aid is often diverted to the government or stolen in route by rebel or criminal groups within the country. The problem becomes particularly acute when there is ongoing unrest and conflict in the country. In this type of setting, humanitarian aid is accused of not only being ineffective, but also of promoting conflict.

Nunn and Qian do a careful econometric analysis of the issue. They find that food aid increases the *duration* of civil wars in countries that have a history of internal conflict. They find no evidence that food aid *starts* civil wars or wars with neighboring countries. This suggests that, during civil wars, the combatants divert the food to soldiers and away from the population in general. Thus, just as with other types of aid, the country-specific situation must be right for aid to have a chance of working in the way the donors intend.

Reforming Foreign Aid

The lack of a positive effect of foreign aid on the growth of developing countries has been disappointing. What can be done to improve aid effectiveness?

Needed: Accountants Without Borders

Countries at all stages of development need to use accounting systems and reliable information flows as a way of constraining political behavior. To have a chance to deal with the tendency to redistribute wealth across generations, rich countries need to institutionalize improved accounting and competing assessments of policy, as is provided by the CBO. The need for an improved accounting system to create government transparency is even greater in poor countries that are in the early stages of developing their government institutions. Development economists view reliable accounting as an essential step to good governance. Paul Collier (2009, p. 214), for example, makes improved government accounting one of his foundational proposals for increasing growth in poor countries:

> Public revenue will leak wherever there is a hole, so there is a large preliminary task of overhauling the practical processes by which money is spent; budgets need accountants, and lots of them. Starting from a culture in which there is no presumption of honesty, the system of financial checks needs to mirror the paranoia of the dictatorships: there needs to be so much interlocking monitoring that even if a few accountants are prepared to be corrupt, they cannot make a difference.

He argues that sound accounting is so essential to effective aid that some independent verification of a country's accounting system by the international community should be a *pre-condition* for aid support.

Alternative Pre-conditions for Aid

The underdevelopment of transparent accounting and evaluation systems is likely an important reason for the lack of correlation between aid and growth. What should be done until a transparent accounting system is developed?

Individual countries and international institutions place or negotiate *conditions* that dictate the way that aid funds are to be used, usually with the hope of jump-starting growth. However, if the use of funds cannot be tracked, then aid effectively becomes *unconditional budget support* that can be used in any way the recipient government sees fit. In many settings, this means the aid will not be used in a manner that permanently raises the living standard of the average citizen.

A better substitute for the lack of transparent accounting in developing countries is to use a *selectivity rule* as a temporary or alternative *pre-condition* for aid support. A developing country should only receive international aid after it has established some track record of domestic policies that have increased growth and reduced poverty. International donors could evaluate the growth records of developing countries and deliver unconditional aid to extend domestic initiatives or policy reforms based on observed early outcomes. Explicitly using country track records should also help reduce the tendency to favor countries for geo-political purposes.

Multilateral Aid

Some interpret the historical record as evidence that donors, especially in the case of individual countries, are not actually interested in generating growth in developing countries. Rather, as suggested above, the aid is used to purchase regional influence as part of a broader geo-political strategy, such as checking a competing superpower, getting access to oil reserves and important mineral sources, making peace in the Middle East, or allowing a military base to be established.

However, rich countries do not have to be sincerely altruistic to want economic growth in developing countries. Growth in poor countries that reduces worldwide income inequality can reduce terrorism and illegal migration flows and increase the world demand for goods. The fact that these benefits from poor country growth are to some degree public goods to rich countries is one reason that aid should flow through international institutions such as the World Bank. Channeling aid through the World Bank should also help mediate the use of aid to advance the interests of anyone donor country.[9]

While aid flowing through the World Bank may help focus the intended purpose of aid, there still remains the necessary cooperation of the recipient countries. Much of the aid during the disappointing post-WWII period was delivered through multilateral international organizations. Even altruistic aid can be diverted away from the intended purpose in a variety of ways, which is why transparent accounting in the recipient countries and selectivity rules remain important.

[9] Clemens and Kremer (2016).

A Knowledge Bank of Development Projects

The World Bank's most useful role in creating growth could be in providing technical assistance and policy advice to developing countries with solid pro-growth leadership. To serve this role best, the Bank should commit to becoming a "knowledge bank."[10] This means increasing its research component to conduct detailed policy evaluation, cost-benefit analysis of specific investment projects, and design of transparent accounting systems. This emphasis is analogous to giving technocrats in the accounting and evaluation offices of domestic governments a bigger role in policy determination. The Bank, and other international institutions, should focus on establishing evidence identifying growth policies and investment projects that work best and then market these ideas to developing countries that are willing to listen.

Along these lines, the USA has recently passed foreign aid legislation that attempts to improve the monitoring and evaluation of aid projects. An important feature of the legislation is to place greater reliance on government technocrats. The Government Accountability Office is to serve as an independent and objective evaluator of the aid process and project results. The goal is to determine what aid projects work and why.[11]

Deal with Corruption First

One aspect of technical assistance is to help developing countries establish an accounting system that can effectively track and tax income and sales. A poor country cannot fund the needed public infrastructure projects on its own without a reliable revenue source. However, helping a developing country reduce tax evasion, without first addressing corruption, is a bad idea. Technical assistance should first focus on keeping track of how the available government funds are used.

Ivanyna et al. (2021) develop growth models that include both corruption and tax evasion, so they can be used to examine the interaction between the two illegal activities. The models reveal that only lowering tax evasion causes tax rates and tax revenue to increase, creating greater opportunities to divert public funds through corruption. The reduction in private disposable income from the higher taxes lowers private capital accumulation and the increase in corruption lowers public investment. The reduction in the private and public capital stocks causes worker productivity and the welfare of private households to fall. Improving the tax system and cracking down on tax evasion may be welfare-improving but only after checks on corruption are made sufficiently strong. If diversion of public funds is made difficult, then lower evasion and higher tax revenue can raise public investment significantly.

---

[10] Clemens and Kremer (2016) and Ravallion (2016).

[11] Ingram (2016).

Appendix

Basic Model

The basic model of immigration assumes (i) all workers are substitutes for each other and (ii) physical capital and technology are fixed. The assumptions of this approach are captured by the textbook Cobb-Douglas production function

$$Y = AK^{\alpha}L^{1-\alpha},$$

where Y denotes the goods and services produced, K the physical capital stocks, L the number of workers employed, and A the productivity index that includes the influence, among other things, of the current quality and types of the physical capital goods and the ideas about how to organize production.

In this model, the demand for labor is determined by the marginal product of labor (MPL)

$$MPL = (1-\alpha)A\left(\frac{K}{L}\right)^{\alpha},$$

which indicates the additional output associated with hiring an additional worker. Firms that maximize profit will hire workers up to the point where the MPL is equal to the market wage.

Holding A and K fixed, immigration increases L. If these additional workers are hired, the MPL will fall, so the wage must first fall to encourage the firm to expand employment. In other words, the greater supply of labor causes a movement down along the labor demand curve until the market wage is low enough to clear the labor market. The supply curve shift is caused by immigration and lowers wages for all workers, according to the basic model.

As discussed in the text, the standard view of immigration does *not* account for possible increases in A or K. An increase in A or K raises the MPL, "shifts up the demand for labor," and raises wages. Evidence indicates that immigration raises both A and K.

Production with Heterogeneous Labor

An alternative to the basic model assumes that workers do *different* production tasks. The worker doing one production task can complement or raise the productivity of workers doing other tasks. An example of a production function that captures complementary labor inputs is

$$Y = AQ^{\alpha}(L^{s})^{1-\alpha},$$

where

$$Q = \theta L^{u} + (1-\theta)BK$$

L^u unskilled labor
L^s skilled labor
θ parameter gauging relative important of labor and machines
B productivity enhancements in physical capital productivity alone

In this production function L^u and K are *substitute* inputs in production while L^s and Q are *complementary* inputs (implying that skilled and unskilled labor are complementary inputs).

We can derive the marginal product for the two types of labor to see how the different inputs interact to affect wages. Define total employment and the capital-labor ratio as $L = L^u + L^s$ and $k = K/L$. For unskilled labor we have

$$\mathrm{MPL}^{u} = \alpha\theta A\left(\frac{(L^{s}/L)}{\theta(L^{u}/L) + (1-\theta)Bk}\right)^{1-\alpha}.$$

Changes that *lower* the marginal product and wages of unskilled labor are (i) *increases* in the unskilled-labor share, the capital-labor ratio, or the productivity of physical capital and (ii) *decreases* in the skilled-labor share.

For skilled labor we have

$$\mathrm{MPL}^{s} = (1-\alpha)A\left(\frac{\theta(L^{u}/L) + (1-\theta)Bk}{(L^{s}/L)}\right)^{\alpha}.$$

Changes that *lower* the marginal product and wages of skilled labor are (i) *increases* in the skilled labor share and (ii) *decreases* in the unskilled-labor share, the capital-labor ratio, or the productivity of physical capital.

The important point is that immigration can increase, decrease, or not affect wages and wage inequality depending on how it affects the shares of skilled and unskilled labor. Immigration must significantly raise L^u/L to lower wages of unskilled labor and increase in wage inequality. This has not been the case in the USA.

What Has Caused the Rise in Inequality?

It is also interesting to note that an increase in B increases wage inequality by lowering wages of unskilled workers and raising the wages of skilled workers—

what is known as *skill-biased technological change*. Increases in B have been an important driver of the increase in US wage inequality since 1980. The increases have been caused by advancement in computing technology and artificial intelligence. Many of these innovations have *substituted* for tasks previously done by unskilled labor. As discussed in Chap. 3, the solution to the inequality challenge is to increase targeted vocational training that gives workers, without 4-year college degrees, the skills they need to *complement* the new technologies in production. Workers need to improve, program, maintain, and repair the "robots" that are replacing them on assembly lines.

References

Alden, E., 2022, "Border Enforcement Won't Solve the US Migrant Crisis," *Council on Foreign Relations*, October 17.

Amiti, M., Redding, S., and Weinstein, D., 2019, "The Impact of the 2018 Tariffs on Prices and Welfare," *Journal of Economic Perspectives*, 33, 187–210.

Baldwin, R., 1992, "Measurable Dynamic Gains from Trade," *Journal of Political Economy*, 100, 162–174.

Bilgin, M., Gozgor, G., and Rangazas, P., 2021, "Immigration, Innovation, and Economic Growth," *Singapore Economic Review*, 66, 685–699.

Bloom, N., Handley, K., Kurman, A., Luck, P., 2019, "The Impact of Chinese Trade on US Employment: The Good, The Bad, and The Debatable," *American Economic Association Annual Meetings*.

Bond, E., Crucini, M., Rodgrigue, J., and Potter, T., 2013, "Misallocation and Productivity Effects of the Smoot-Hawley Tariff," *Review of Economic Dynamics*, 161, 120–134.

Borjas, G., Freeman, R., and Katz, L., 1997, "How Much do Immigration and Trade affect Labor Market Outcomes?" *Brookings Papers on Economic Activity*, 1–67.

Burstein, A., Morales, E., and Vogel, J., 2019, "Changes in Between-Group Inequality: Computers, Occupations, and International Trade," *American Economics Journal: Macroeconomics*, 11, 348–400.

Broda, C., and Weistein, D., 2006, "Globalization and the Gains from Variety," *Quarterly Review of Economics*, 121, 541–585.

Caliendo, L., Dvorkin, M., and Parro, F., 2019, "Trade and Labor Market Dynamics: General Equilibrium Analysis of the China Trade Shock," *Econmetrica*, 87, 741–835.

Chatzky, A., McBride, J., and Sergie, M., 2020, "NAFTA and the USMCA: Weighing the Impact of North American Trade," *Council on Foreign Relations*, July1.

Clemens, M., and Kremer, M., 2016, "The New Role for the World Bank," *Journal of Economic Perspectives*, 30, 53–76.

Collier, P., 2009, *War, Guns, and Votes*, New York: Harper Collins.

Das, S., Mourmouras, A., and Rangazas, P., 2018, *Economic Growth and Development: A Dynamic Dual Economy Approach*, New York: Springer.

Easterly, W., Levine, R., and Roodman, D., 2004, "Aid, Policies, and Growth," *American Economic Review*, 94, 774–780.

Fajgelbaum, P., and Khandelwal, A., 2022, "The Economic Impacts of the US-China Trade War," *Annual Review of Economics*, 14, 1–29.

Fajgelbaum, P., Goldberg, P., Kennedy, P., and Khandelwal, A., 2020, "The Return to Protectionism," *Quarterly Journal of Economics*, 135, 1–55.

Feenstra, R., 2018, "Restoring the Product Variety and Pro-competitive Gains from Trade with Heterogenous Firms and Bounded Productivity," *Journal of International Economics*, 110, 16–17.

———., 2010, *Product Variety and the Gains from International Trade*, Cambridge, MA: MIT Press.

Feenstra, R., and Hanson, R., 1999, "The Impact of Outsourcing and High-Technology Capital on Wages: Estimates for the US, 1979–1990, *Quarterly Economic Journal*, 114, 907–940.

Feenstra, R., and Kee, H., 2008, "Export Variety and Country Productivity: Estimating the Monopolistic Competition Model with Endogenous Productivity," *Journal of International Economics*, 74, 500–518.

Feenstra, R. and Weinstein, D., 2017, "Globalization, Markups, and US Welfare," *Journal of Political Economy*, 125, 1040–1074.

Foged, M., Hasager, L., and Peri, G., 2022, "Comparing the Effects of Policies for the Labor Market Integration of Refugees," *NBER Working Paper* 30534.

Freenstra, R., 2015, *Advanced International Trade: Theory and Evidence*, Second Edition, Princeton: Princeton University Press.

Helpman, E., 2018, *Globalization and Inequality*, Cambridge, MA: Harvard University Press.

Hunt, J., and Gauthier-Loiselle, M., 2010, "How Much does Immigration Boost Innovation?" *American Economics Journal: Macroeconomics*, 2, 31–56.

Ingram, G., 2016, "Congress finds Bipartisan Support for Aid and Aid Reform," *Future Development: Economics to End Poverty*, Washington: Brookings Institution.

Irwin, D., 2005, "Welfare Effects of Autarky: Evidence from the Jeffersonian Embargo of 1807–1809," *Review of International Economics*, 13, 631–645.

Ivanyna, M., Mourmouras, A., and Rangazas, P., 2021, *The Macroeconomics of Corruption: Governance and Growth*, New York: Springer.

Katz, L. and Murphy, K., 1992, "Changes in Relative Wages 1963-1987: Supply and Demand Factors," *Quarterly Economic Review*, 107, 35–78.

Klobucista, C., Cheatham, A., and Roy, D., 2022, "The US Immigration Debate," *Council on Foreign Relations Backgrounder*, August 3.

Krueger, A., 2022, "The False Promise of America's Chips Act," *Project Syndicate*.

Leamer, E., 1998, "In Search of Stopler-Samuelson Linkages between Trade and Lower Wages," in S.Collins, editor, *Imports, Exports, and the American Worker*, Washington: Brookings Institution Press.

Mitchener, K., O'Rourke, K., and Wandschneider, K., 2021, "The Smoot-Hawley Trade War," NBER Working Paper No. 28616.

Nunn, N., and Qian, N., 2014, "US Food Aid and Civil Conflict," *American Economic Review*, 104, 1630–1666.

Ossa, R., 2015, "Why Trade Matters After All," *Journal of International Economics*, 97, 266–277.

Peri, G., 2022, "Immigration Swan Song," *Finance and Development*, Washington DC: IMF

———, 2016, "Immigration, Productivity, and Labor Markets," *Journal of Economic Perspectives*, 30, 3–30.

Rajan, R., and Subramanian, A., 2011, "Aid, Dutch Disease, and Manufacturing," *Journal of Development Economics*, 94, 106–118.

———, 2008 "Aid and Growth: What Does the Cross-Country Evidence Really Show?" *Review of Economics and Statistics*, 90, 643–665.

Ravallion, M., 2016, "The World Bank: Why it is Still Needed and Why it Still Disappoints," *Journal of Economic Perspectives*, 30, 77–94.

Ting-Fang, C., 2022, "TSMC Founder Morris Chang says Globalization Almost Dead," *Nikkei Asia*, December 8.

Wadhwa, V., 2012, *The Immigrant Exodus*, Philadelphia: Wharton Digital Press.
World Bank, 2023, "Exports of Goods and Services (% of GDP)," Worldbank.org/indicator/NE.EXP.GNFS.ZS
Wright, G., 2014, "Revisiting the Employment Impact of Offshoring," *European Economic Review*, 66, 63–83.

Chapter 5
Climate Policy

The climate is changing and mostly due to human activity. The change is the result of an accumulation of several gases in our atmosphere such as water vapor, methane, nitrous oxides, chlorofluorocarbons, and carbon dioxide (CO_2). These "greenhouse" gases absorb and emit radiation that heats the earth surface. The greenhouse gas with the greatest impact on the warming of the earth is CO_2, a gas that results from the burning of fossil fuels (coal, oil, and natural gas).

Increasing population and worker productivity for more than two centuries has raised GDP and the burning of fossil fuels. For example, in the USA, GDP grew about 3% annually over the twentieth century and as a result emitted 1.5% more CO_2 into the atmosphere every year (Nordhaus 2013, pp. 19–23). The emissions of CO_2 grew more slowly than GDP because for most of the twentieth century the CO_2 intensity of our economy (CO_2/GDP) has fallen due primarily to more energy-efficient production across sectors, a shift to service sectors and away from the more energy intensive manufacturing, and a shift away from carbon-intensive fuels toward less carbon-intensive fuels and non-fossil fuel sources of energy. The gains in energy efficiency are encouraging because they have happened without any significant push from government policy. However, while the efficiency of our energy use has improved, it has not been enough to keep emissions from rising due to economic growth. In addition, what really matters is what is happening at the global level. In the last half century, world GDP grew faster than in the USA and the decline in CO_2 intensity was less sharp, resulting in an average annual increase in emissions of 2.6%. A significant global policy initiative will be needed to limit emissions and the resulting rise in temperature.

Scientists form baseline projections of the CO_2 growth over the twenty-first century based on the counterfactual assumption (we hope) that no policies will be passed to limit or constrain CO_2 emissions. This approach to forming projections is needed to inform and inspire the need for policy action, in the same way, and for the

© The Author(s), under exclusive license to Springer Nature Switzerland AG 2023
A. Mourmouras, P. Rangazas, *US Economic Policy in the 21st Century*,
Professional Practice in Governance and Public Organizations,
https://doi.org/10.1007/978-3-031-36437-2_5

same reasons, that forecasts of the fiscal gap and public debt ratios are made (see Chap. 2). Following Nordhaus (2013) again, the projections estimate a continued annual growth of CO_2 emissions in a range between 0.5% and 2% annually.

Recent estimates of the actual growth in CO_2 emissions are roughly consistent with the projected range estimated by Nordhaus 10 years ago. The average annual growth rate for emissions was 2.6% for 2000–2009 and 1.5% for 2010–2019.[1] Revisions have been made by some scientists, based an adjusted estimates of the contribution of land use to emissions, that have lowered the growth rate over the last decade to approximately zero.[2] While encouraging, it is too early to know if the downward revision was due to lasting changes in land use policy or whether land use improvements will continue to offset the burning of fossil fuels that are pushing CO_2 emissions higher.

The economic consequences of rising CO_2 concentration in the atmosphere stems from the resulting rise in global temperatures. While sustained economic growth began with the early stages of the Industrial Revolution around 1800, the climate impact of expanding production was not evident until the beginning of the twentieth century. The temperature rise after 1900, what is often referred to as the rise above pre-industrial levels, receives the most attention. Global temperatures have risen almost 1.0 °C or almost 1.8 °F over the twentieth century. Most climate models predict that, without significant policy change or unforeseen dramatic technological development, the 2100 global temperature will exceed the 1900 level by between 2.0 and 4 °C or 3.5 and 7.5 °F. Changes in these ranges have the potential to cause much higher seal levels, increased hurricanes of greater intensity, and more droughts and wildfires.

Major coordinated international policy actions to address climate change have not yet occurred, but there is increasing attention devoted to the issue. The Paris Agreement in 2015, a legally binding treaty involving almost 200 countries, set a goal of limiting global warming to a range of 1.5–2.0 °C above pre-industrial levels. Limiting temperature increases to this range would require *decreases* in the level of CO_2, *negative* annual growth rates in emissions (Tirole 2017, Figure 8.1). While important symbolically, the Paris Agreement does not require participating countries to meet enforceable emissions standards. The contribution of individual countries toward meeting the agreed upon goal through changes in domestic policy is strictly voluntary. Nordhaus (2018, 2021) argues that policy is nowhere near what is needed to limit the temperature rise to 2.0 °C over the century.

The USA originally signed on to the Paris Agreement but US involvement was removed under the Trump administration. Trump also rolled back emissions standards and other domestic policies put in place under Obama to limit the carbon footprint of the USA. President Biden has recommitted the USA to the goals of the Paris Agreement, removed many of the Trump rollbacks, and set a goal of net zero

[1] Based on data from Ritchie et al. (2020).

[2] Hausfather (2021).

carbon emissions by 2050. Net zero emissions means that carbon emissions do not exceed the carbon naturally absorbed and stored by forests, oceans, and soils or potentially captured by new technologies. This ambitious goal would be a good start but remember that level of CO_2 must be *reduced* to meet the temperature targets.

The Climate Change Target

Where did the goal of limiting global warming to a range of 1.5–2.0 °C come from? There is a scientific basis for limiting warming within this range. Scientists have estimated that beyond this range, there is an increasing probability of creating instability in the earth's system, resulting in sharp discontinuities or "tipping points" in the planet's behavior. Once the planet warms beyond 2°, the loss of alpine glaciers, the Greenland ice sheet, and the West Antarctic ice sheet becomes a real possibility. The deglaciation of the Northern Hemisphere would cause significant elevation of sea levels, threatening the survival of coastal cities and island nations. If temperatures rise beyond 4°, the permafrost begins to thaw. This is a particularly scary tipping point because vast amounts of carbon would be released into the atmosphere creating a feedback effect that would accelerate global warming.

While the current target may be defensible on scientific grounds, some would argue that it is already infeasible given the lack of aggressive policy action and our current technologies for controlling carbon emissions. In his base case with no policy change and with energy efficiency gains in line with historical trends, Nordhaus (2018) estimates that global temperatures will be 4.0 °C above 1900 levels by 2100. Climate Analytics estimates an increase in temperature in the 2.0°–3.6° range, with a median estimate of 2.7, assuming the world does no better than its current climate policy stance.[3]

Economic Effects of Climate Change

The difficult job of estimating the economic consequences of climate change requires linking the predictions about temperature change to the impact on the natural world (average temperatures, sea levels, ocean acidity, hurricane frequency and intensity, droughts, and wildfires) and then relating those physical changes to effects on human welfare. The human effects arise from changes in agricultural output, the health environment, property values, and the wildlife that people value. A dollar value is attached to each of these human effects and the total dollar loss is expressed as a fraction of GDP. In short, the challenging exercise involves

[3] Climate Action Tracker (2021).

calculating the dollar valuation of the permanent loss in welfare caused by a given increase in temperature. The economic effects of climate change are much more uncertain than the physical effects, which are quite uncertain in their own right.

Based on Nordhaus (2013, 2018), a 2.5 °C rise in temperature, a reasonable lower bound for the rise over this century, is estimated to cause a *permanent annual welfare loss* equivalent to 1.5% of global GDP. This is a counterfactual calculation that attempts to answer the question, "How much lower would GDP be if we lived in a world that was 2.5 °C warmer?" As temperature gradually increases over several decades to the ultimate 2.5 °C rise, the loss in each decade would be increasing but would be smaller than the estimated 1.5% loss in global GDP. The estimated losses rise sharply with further increases in temperature. If temperatures rise by an additional half degree to reach 3.0 °C, the ultimate annual loss in global output is estimated to be 2%. A rise of one degree more to reach 4.0 °C doubles the global output loss to 4%.

It is also important to note that the costs of global warming vary significantly across geographical location and a country's stage of development, causing losses in particular locations to differ from the average global decline. For example, as temperatures rise in Africa, where the (too) warm climate already results in low agricultural productivity and unhealthy environments, food production and water availability could be severely compromised. The coastal areas in Asia will see flooding as sea levels rise. Central America will face the brunt of hurricane intensification. In contrast, countries in colder climates with greater land mass away from the coast will not face similar risks. In addition, richer and technologically advanced economies can more easily adapt to rising temperatures in ways that minimize the cost—changes in farm technologies, preventive health care responses, more air conditioning at work and home, migration of businesses and residents away from coastal areas, and creation of flood barriers. The welfare loss will be a much larger percent of GDP in the developing countries of Africa, Asia, and South American than in Europe and the USA, both because of the uneven damages of climate change and differing capabilities to adapt.[4] One implication is that increasing economic development of poor countries is one way of reducing the global cost of climate change. For this reason, simply reducing economic growth is not the best way to reduce emissions and limit temperature change.

The economic costs of allowing climate change to occur unabated are significant, especially in locations vulnerable to sea level and temperature increases. Reducing carbon emissions associated with economic activity is certainly not impossible. Rather than reducing emissions by slowing economic growth, the focus should be on changing how we consume and produce goods and services. The first step in developing a policy response to climate change is to understand the economic costs of a warmer planet and then balance those against the cost of changing behavior and production methods to limit carbon emissions.

---

[4]Bannister and Mourmouras (2017) estimate the effects of climate change on global and income and welfare convergence.

The Marginal Social Cost of Carbon Emissions

Given the significant costs associated with climate change, what would be an achievable target or perhaps even an *optimal* achievable target for carbon emissions that would guide climate policy action? The economic notion of an optimal target balances the expected costs of temperature increases against the costs of limiting those increases by reducing emissions. Once determining a target for emissions, there is then the issue of what new policy will get us there.

The economic approach to climate change is to view the policy response as a grand public policy project. To assess the value of a public project, a cost-benefit analysis is done that estimates the marginal benefits against the marginal costs of the required public expenditures. The optimal level of expenditures is where the marginal benefits (which typically decline with the level of expenditures) just balance against the marginal costs (which typically rise with the level of expenditures) of additional expenditures.

In the context of climate policy, the cost-benefit analysis applies to policy actions that limit the level of CO_2 emissions and the associated rise in global temperature. The first job is to assess the marginal costs or marginal economic damages caused by allowing an additional rise in emissions, what we call the marginal social cost of emissions (MSC). This cost must be balanced against the marginal abatement cost of reducing emissions (MAC), the value of lost production of goods and services associated with limiting a further rise in emissions. Estimates suggest that the MSC rises and the MAC falls with the total level or concentration of emissions. This means allowing additional emissions is more damaging and the abatement costs associated with limiting those emissions are lower when the level of emissions is already high. If at the current level of CO_2 concentration in the atmosphere, the MSC of allowing additional emissions is greater than the MAC of preventing them, then society would be better off if we took actions to decrease emissions. We begin by discussing the MSC of emissions in this section and then turn to the MAC in the next section.

Estimating the MSC of a given amount of CO_2 emissions is even harder than the job of answering the static counterfactual question of how much lower global GDP would be if we lived in a world with higher temperatures. This is because the MSC is the present value of the rise in social costs at every point in time into the indefinite future (the additional CO_2 will stay in the atmosphere for a long time). Estimating the path of the rise in costs from more emissions today is challenging. In addition, to compare the future costs to the current cost of preventing emissions requires that the *present value* of the future costs be computed. The *discount factor* (or interest rate) used to compute the present value of the future costs matters quite a bit, creating an important reason why MSC estimates vary.

Economists typically think of the discount factor as being determined by the opportunity cost of funds. For example, the fundamental value of a stock is estimated by discounting the expected stream of dividends from owning the stock. For the discount rate, you might use the interest rate on long-term corporate debt that you could purchase instead of the stock. In the climate change context, you can think of investing a dollar of current resources to raise the real income of future generations by lowering current CO_2 emissions and the related future economic damages. Alternatively, you could invest that same dollar of resources into physical or human capital formation that would also raise the income of future generations. From this perspective, you should use the rate of return to investment in physical or human capital, typically estimated to be between 5% and 10% annually, to form the discount rate. There is also the complication that the return to alternative investments in capital decreases over time as capital accumulates (recall from earlier chapters that diminishing returns cause the rate of return to capital to fall).

Some economists argue for a lower discount rate than the those based on the marginal return to physical or human capital investments. One argument is that the return to investments in physical and human capital are risky because they will vary with conditions that affect the productivity of capital and labor used to make goods and services (such as the recent pandemic or geopolitical events that alter the how goods are made and traded). Part of the average return to investments in physical and human capital reflects a *risk premium* that compensates investors for possible fluctuations in returns due to unpredictable changes in economic conditions. Investments that limit climate change may yield output gains that are not as sensitive to these conditions and thus are less risky. If this is true, then investments in climate control should be compared to less risky investments such as government debt that pay lowers returns (Wagner and Weitzman 2015, pp. 70–74). Another argument is that it is *unethical* to discount the damages to future generations at all, suggesting a discount rate closer to zero (Stern 2006). Thus, even if you could reliably estimate the rise in temperature caused by additional CO_2 emitted today, and the associated economic damages over time, you could still debate the appropriate value for the discount factor when computing the MSC.

We think that if one is going to look at climate change in terms of its economic consequences, then it is reasonable to view it as an investment that can raise output, consumption, and welfare just as with other investments. In addition, the costs of climate change are likely to vary with the same conditions that affect overall productivity. This means investment in climate change prevention yields returns with risk that are similar to those associated with economic investment in capital.

For example, the economic losses of flooding, hurricanes, and droughts are larger, the greater is the potential production that was disrupted by these events. Even the economic loss in plant and animal species and other aspects of the environment are likely to be larger in more productive economies because when the economic value humans placed on such losses are likely to be greater, the higher is the consumption. People worry more about species loss and are willing to pay more to avoid them, the farther they are from subsistence consumption levels that threaten their own survival. The amount that an individual is willing to pay to avoid the loss of poison dart frogs or polar bears increases with consumption levels. Thus, the benefit of climate change investment will be positively correlated with the benefits from economic investment. For these reasons, we follow the approach used by Nordhaus and most other climate researchers in using the return to physical capital when discounting the costs and benefits of investments in climate control.

Table 5.1 The MSC of carbon emissions (2010 dollars per ton of carbon)

	Nordhaus	EPA
2020	$35.7	$44.2
2030	$49.5	$52.6
2050	$98.3	$72.6

Nordhaus has computed the MSC over several decades, constantly refining estimates of the rise in global temperatures, the likely impact on the natural world, and the resulting economic consequences. Nordhaus (2018) contains his most recent estimates, presented in Table 5.1 along with estimates computed by the Environmental Protection Agency (EPA 2016). These estimates are formed based on the assumption of no major climate policy changes throughout the century. The MSC is computed for three different years 2020, 2030, and 2050. Note the MSC rises over time. This is because, as mentioned above, when the additional costs created by one more ton of CO_2 emissions is greater, the higher the level of CO_2 concentrated in the atmosphere. As CO_2 concentrations and global temperatures rise, the cost of further emissions also rises.

Nordhaus and the EPA use different discount rates in their calculations. Based on estimates of the return to physical capital, Nordhaus assumes the discount rate is 5.1% initially and then falls over time to 3.6%, with an average value of 4.25%. The EPA uses a constant discount rate of 3%.

The Nordhaus and EPA values computed for 2020 and for 2030 are similar, with the lower value computed by Nordhaus at least partially explained by the higher discount rate assumed. Going out to 2050, the MSC increases dramatically especially when estimated by Nordhaus, despite the higher discount rate he used. It must that the EPA estimates a smaller rise in temperature or smaller economic costs for a given increase in temperature.

The Marginal Abatement Cost of Limiting Climate Change

The MAC or marginal costs of limiting climate change is the income the economy must sacrifice to reduce CO_2 emissions by one ton. This is measured by considering the costs of changing production and use of energy in ways that reduce emissions, for example, producing electricity using natural gas rather than coal (the major CO_2 emitting energy source) or driving more fuel-efficient cars. Naturally, these costs are dependent on the available technologies for energy production. The development of cleaner technologies would reduce the MAC, and government action toward this end should be part of climate policy.

For the currently available production technologies, as one considers reducing emissions by greater amounts, the marginal costs of abatement rise. For example, the costs of converting an electricity power plant from coal to natural gas may be relatively low, especially if it is an older coal plant that needs to be replaced anyway. However, natural gas still emits CO_2. To reduce emissions further would require a more expensive investment and more costly electricity production using renewable energy sources such as wind or solar. Reducing emissions from driving is considered more costly than the switch from coal to natural gas electrical plants. More fuel-efficient cars reduce emissions at relatively low cost but further reductions in emissions requires a switch to electric cars powered by renewable energy, requiring large investments and more costly transportation services. To drive emissions to zero with today's technologies would be quite expensive. Nordhaus (2018) estimates that moving to zero emissions would require a drop in output and income of 7.4%.

For these reasons, total abatement costs are estimated to be a convex function of the abatement rate, the fraction of emissions that are reduced. The parameters of the abatement cost function are calibrated to match the estimated costs of achieving different emission targets. The convex shape implies that the MAC is an increasing function of the level of emissions abated.

The Optimal Level of Carbon Emissions

The optimal level of carbon emissions minimizes the sum of economic damages from the associated temperature rise plus the economic costs of limiting the emissions. The total costs are minimized at the emission level where the MSC equals the MAC. At emission levels below this point, the MSC is less than the MAC and increasing emissions will lower the total cost to the world. At emission levels above this point, the MSC is greater than the MAC suggesting a decrease in emissions would lower total costs.

Nordhaus (2018) estimates that the optimal level of carbon emissions would limit temperature rise by 2100 to 3.5 °C. This is significantly higher than the goal of a 2.0 °C rise. However, it would still require a climate policy push because he estimates that if we continue on a business-as-usual (BAU) path with no significant policy change, the temperature increase will be 4.0 °C by the end of the century. Achieving the much more ambitious climate targets currently discussed will require a policy push that may be too costly according to Nordhaus's calculations.

Recent estimates computed by Bannister and Mourmouras (2017) and Ivanyna and Mourmouras (2023) provide estimates on the net costs of meeting the Paris Agreement to limit the temperature rise to a 2.0 °C that reach a different conclusion. They compute the welfare losses from global CO_2 emissions, based on evidence from historical temperature shocks, on the expected utility over the life of a representative household in each country. The welfare costs of CO_2 emissions are first calculated under BAU assumption, which assumes that global emissions remain on their current path. Under BAU, emissions lead to higher temperatures and lower output and consumption. The measured effects are country-specific because the negative effects from rising temperatures and changing precipitation have an empirical relationship with a country's GDP and geographic location.

Across the globe, the study finds that climate change lowers welfare. In doing their calculations, the authors consider the uncertainty associated with climate projections. For example, some climate models predict that the earth will be much warmer in 2050 under the BAU baseline. Households in the model have risk averse preferences, and the uncertain nature of climate change adds a quantitatively important dimension to expected utility and welfare calculations. Uncertainty over climate change is rising over time, exerting a larger negative effect on welfare through this mechanism. A major motivation for policies seeking to limit global warming is to provide insurance against potentially bad outcomes that raise uncertainty and lower welfare.

Welfare effects are also computed assuming that a carbon tax is used to lower emissions consistent with the temperature rise target set under the Paris Agreement. The carbon tax *rate* is the same in all countries, but the *total* tax paid depends on country-specific emission levels. The tax collected is spread across the country's population to compute the reduction in average consumption. Despite the carbon tax, the Paris Agreement scenario generally dominates the BAU scenario in overall welfare. This is in contrast to the Nordhaus conclusion that average welfare would be lower under a 2.0 °C target.

There is considerable geographic variation in welfare changes associated with the comparison of the Paris Agreement versus BAU. At one extreme, welfare *declines* by 12% under cold and carbon-intensive Mongolia. At the other extreme, it *rises* by 21% in the hot and carbon-light Bahamas. Regionally, welfare under the Paris Agreement exceeds that under BAU in all areas except Emerging and Developing Europe, where emissions are high and the benefit of lower temperature is small. The warm climates in the MENA and East Asia regions create a net gain despite the high carbon taxes collected there. Latin America, the Caribbean, the USA, and sub-Saharan Africa incur the largest net welfare gain under the Paris Agreement.

Climate Policy in Theory

The insights of economic theory are fundamental to understanding why climate policy is needed and what form it might take. Introductory economics teaches us that markets fail to efficiently allocate resources in the presence of *externalities*—byproducts of economic activity that cause benefits or damages to those not directly involved in the market transactions. Negative externalities are external damages or *social* costs that are not included in the market prices that reflect only the *private* costs associated with producing a good or service. In the presence of negative externalities, market prices are too low from a social perspective causing too much of the goods to be produced and traded; a misallocation of resources that lowers overall welfare.

Climate change is associated with particularly difficult externalities. First, the damages caused by climate change are hard to estimate or even fully imagine. Second, the worst damages will occur far into the future, impacting young and unborn generations. Third, the damages escape not just economic transactions or local communities but entire countries, affecting everyone on earth with disproportionate damages occurring in poor countries that do not generate most of the CO_2 emissions.

Theory tells us that we can efficiently reduce the pace of global warming by internalizing the social cost associated with CO_2 emissions. Decision-makers involved in economic activity that generates emissions need to confront not only the private resource cost of the activity but also the social cost. This requires that the MSC caused by the CO_2 emitted when one unit of the good is produced and used must be "priced" so that the social cost is internalized by buyers and sellers in the same way that the marginal private cost is reflected in market prices. Each decision-maker participating in the market for goods that involve CO_2 emissions would then make choices about how to produce the good and how much of the good to use based on the adjusted price and their assessment of how costly it would be to change their behavior (i.e., based on their own assessment of the MAC).

Ideally, the pricing of carbon would be linked to the MSC estimates from Table 5.1 above. About 0.00889 tons of CO_2 is emitted per gallon of gas burned. So, if the carbon dioxide emissions were priced at say $50 per ton, the marginal costs of using a gallon of gas would be about 44 cents higher. The higher price of gas would give rise to a variety of market responses that would reduce gas production and consumption and thereby carbon emissions. Similarly, a $50 price of per ton of CO_2 emissions adds about $140 to the price of a ton of coal, more than doubling the cost of electricity made from coal. The higher costs would increase the incentive to transition to natural gas and renewables as energy sources for making electricity.

The way that most economists recommend that carbon be priced is using a sales tax levied on products based on their carbon emissions. A carbon tax would be broad-based, levied on any products releasing carbon emissions. It would raise tax revenue, as suggested in Chap. 2, and would be relatively easy to administer.

Issues in Setting Climate Policy

Pricing carbon emissions based on their MSC provides a foundational approach to deal with climate change. There are various aspects of building on this approach that should at least be considered if global warming is to be limited as efficiently as possible.

Rising Carbon Tax

Any scheme for carbon pricing should be based on the MSC. We know that the greater the additional costs created by one more ton of CO_2 emissions, the higher the level of CO_2 concentrated in the atmosphere. As CO_2 concentrations and global temperatures rise, the cost of further emissions also rises. This explains why the MSC estimates in Table 5.1 increase over time. An efficient carbon tax scheme should be a *schedule* of tax rates that reflect the rising MSC. It also means that the longer we wait to get serious about climate policy, the harder it will be to develop an efficient approach because the required *initial* carbon tax becomes greater, making it more likely to be met with political resistance. As time passes, the chance that the carbon tax is high enough to reflect the MSC diminishes. Another reason is that it makes sense to act *quickly* on imposing a carbon tax schedule.

Carbon Pricing: Carbon Tax vs. Cap and Trade

Pricing carbon emissions can be done in two ways. We have focused on using a carbon tax, which is preferred by most economists. An alternative is for government to issue permits that allow firms to emit a specified amount of carbon dioxide in production. The permits enable the government to "cap" the legal level of total emissions. To create a carbon price via a market mechanism, the permits are "traded" across firms. Producers that do not emit much carbon or that can move to a cleaner production technology at relatively low cost would sell their permits to producers that do not have low-cost clean technology alternatives. Tradable permits results in the same total emissions but at a lower output cost to society. This system is called "cap and trade" or "tradable permits."

For example, imagine a firm that is currently producing electricity with a relatively new coal plant that is not energy efficient in general. It may still have substantial financing costs to repay the debt taken on to build the plant and it may also be in a location where solar and wind power is not reliable. This plant would emit large amounts of carbon in the plant's heating/cooling and lighting as well as in electricity production, with no good current option to reduce emissions. All these considerations suggest the firm will need to purchase a relatively large number of emission permits directly from the government or from other electricity producers that can more easily transition to a more energy-efficient plant that uses natural gas or renewables to produce electricity. The high-carbon emitting firms will drive the price of permits (carbon) up and help convince other producers, in better situations to make the transition toward cleaner energy, to reduce their need for permits.

California has a version of this type of system. The state issues credits to automakers that produce zero emission cars with the goal of reaching a given total number of electric cars produced in the state. *Every* automaker in the state is required to accumulate a certain minimum number of credits (the targeted total of electric cars, and required credits, is divided among the state's automakers). However, the credits are tradable, which means an automaker does not have to receive the credits directly from the state (i.e., does not have to produce electric cars at all). Firms that do not make any electric cars must purchase these credits from firms that produce more than the minimum. A firm is willing to buy credits because to make enough electric cars to receive the credits directly from the state would be too costly.

In California, Tesla receives a large number of credits from the state, way beyond the minimum required of an individual automaker, because it has a viable technology for making electric cars. Tesla then sells the excess credits it acquires from the state to firms that make no electric cars but need to meet the credit minimum. In fact,

Tesla makes hundreds of millions of dollars by selling credits. Tesla is not the only winner. Society is also better off because the cost of achieving the total number of electric cars produced is accomplished at the lowest possible cost, i.e., by encouraging low-cost producers to do the work of reaching the overall target.

The tradable permit approach has the advantage that it is not explicitly a "tax," which may have political advantages, although it essentially works like the carbon tax by creating a price for carbon that drives up the price of goods that emit carbon. By now most politicians and citizens recognize this. Another advantage is that it allows the government to easily target emission levels using the total permit cap. However, while total emissions are predictable, the price of permits (carbon) is not because the demand for permits can change with market conditions (caused by, say, technological innovations or the relative price of different sources of energy). The EU currently operates an emissions trading system where the price of permits has proved to be quite volatile. In contrast, the carbon tax essentially fixes the price of carbon (but not the level of emissions). This has the advantage of creating a more clear and certain incentive to invest in new technologies. The carbon tax approach is also viewed as being easier to administer, especially if you want to include direct incentives for changes in household, as well as firm, behavior.

Costs of Taxation

Using policy to raise the price of carbon, either through a carbon tax or a public auction of carbon permits, increases government revenue. The theory of public finance has developed a concept for the total burden (including the marginal *excess burden* or loss in gains from trade beyond the revenue collected) associated with raising an additional unit of government revenue called the *marginal cost of public funds* (MCPF). The basic results from this literature are that (i) the MCPF exceeds one when *additional* revenue is raised on top of *existing* taxes and (ii) the greater the size of the MCPF, the higher is the level of initial tax rates.[5] In short, there are costs to society in collecting a dollar of tax revenue and the costs rise as tax rates increase.

A full policy analysis of adding carbon pricing should include the complication that governments have existing taxes of various kinds in place. Using the MCPF concept, the level of these existing taxes affects the optimal carbon tax rate.[6] For example, suppose that a government taxes wages. A wage tax reduces real income, beyond the tax revenue collected, by lowering the after-tax wage and discouraging labor supply, employment, and output. Adding a carbon tax reduces the *real* after-tax wage further by raising the price of some market goods that could be purchased with the wages earned and thereby reduces work incentives further. The full additional costs in lost output from the carbon tax are reflected in the MCPF.

[5] See, for example, Boadway and Wildasin (1984, pp. 393–395).
[6] McKitrick (2016, section 3).

For this reason, the optimal carbon tax must be scaled down by the MCPF, causing the tax rate to fall below the MSC. Intuitively, carbon emissions become relatively cheaper once the full burden of discouraging emissions is included. Research has shown that taking the full effects of a carbon tax into account can be quantitatively important. Based on simulations of the US tax system, Bovenberg and Goulder (1996) conclude that the optimal carbon tax is substantially below the MSC. McKitrick (2016) argues that the optimal carbon tax should be about half the MSC in Canada.

One way to restore the principle that the optimal carbon should equal the MSC is to assume that when the carbon tax is levied, other distortionary taxes are lowered to make the policy *revenue neutral*. This could happen in countries that are not in need of tax revenue but countries such as the USA face both a fiscal crisis and a climate crisis. Properly accounting for the MCPF complication also means that the optimal carbon tax, for countries in need of tax revenue, will vary according to the initial level of current taxes. A relatively high tax country such as Canada should have a lower carbon tax than a relatively low tax country such as the USA.

International Dimension

Climate change models such as those developed by Nordhaus and his colleagues and by Ivanyna and Mourmouras (2023) are based on a *global* economy. Estimates of the carbon price needed to meet emission and temperature targets assume the price is applied *uniformly* across the world. A uniform global carbon tax potentially makes sense because climate change is fundamentally a global problem—no matter where emissions occur, the effect on the climate is the same. However, it ignores the fact that dealing with climate change efficiently requires international negotiation and cooperation. Cooperation is made difficult by geopolitical tensions related to issues other than climate change but also more fundamentally by the *free-rider problem. All* countries benefit from a reduction in emissions *anywhere* in the world. This means individual countries have the incentive to shift the burden of meeting emission targets onto other countries. In addition, individual countries contribute to climate change differently and also bear different burdens from a warming planet.

For example, the country creating the most carbon emissions today is China. China is a large economy that still relies heavily on coal as a source of energy. Limiting future emissions becomes much easier if China is part of an agreement to impose a common global price of carbon. However, China can argue that it should not levy the same carbon price as in developed Western countries that were the main source of carbon emissions in the past, that are much richer than China today on a per capita basis, and whose citizens are better able to absorb greater taxation. These fairness and equity considerations will intertwine with the free rider problem to play a part in determining international climate policy.

Consider also the large number of countries that are at lower levels of economic development than China. Low-income countries depend dramatically more on *natural capital* to generate income flows than rich countries. Natural capital is the sum of renewable resources such as agricultural land and forests plus nonrenewable resources such as fossil fuels and minerals. While richer countries have more natural capital than poorer countries, it is a small fraction of their total wealth because they have huge stocks of man-made physical capital and human capital. In low-income countries, natural capital makes up almost 50% of their total wealth, while in rich OECD countries it is only about 3% of total wealth (Lange et al. 2018). The way poor countries make natural capital work to generate current income is to reduce the long-run stocks of nonrenewables (fuels) and renewables (by converting forests into farmland) both of which play a role in raising global temperatures.[7]

Climate change itself will hit many of these poor countries disproportionately hard because they are in warmer climates and because of their heavy reliance on agriculture. However, *preventing* climate change would also hurt them by limiting their ability to use their natural capital to generate current income. A way out of this dilemma is for the richer countries to offer greater support for economic development via physical and human capital accumulation, following the development policy principles we laid out in Chap. 4. Economic development reduces the dependency on natural capital as a source of income and reduces stress on natural resources by reducing fertility and population growth. International climate agreements and development aid must be determined jointly.

Even agreement and coordination of climate policy among rich countries is a challenge. We have seen that the most efficient way to set carbon prices cannot ignore the existing domestic tax policy, which varies dramatically across the world. Subsidies of renewable energy products within countries compromise free trade agreements. Subsidizing basic research in climate change and new technologies must confront the free rider problem. Combining these economic considerations with geopolitical tensions on other issues suggests that achieving a binding international agreement on global climate policy, let alone one that is efficient, will be very difficult.

Carbon Border Tax

As mentioned, the EU has a cap-and-trade system that establishes a market price for carbon emissions. There are complaints that this system puts EU firms at a disadvantage when the EU trades with other countries that do not force their firms to pay

[7] Natural capital is also related to the separate issue of *sustainability*. *Strong* sustainability refers to a situation where the natural capital of a country is being maintained over time. *Weak* sustainability refers to the situation where the total wealth of a country is not falling over time so that consumption can be sustained going forward. Ivanyna and Mourmouras (2023) find that consumption is unsustainable in 69 countries that deplete their national capital and other forms of wealth.

for carbon emissions. These foreign firms can export products to the EU market at a cheaper price. As exports take over a larger market share, the climate change policy of the EU is undermined. This situation also creates incentives for EU firms to offshore and avoid the domestic carbon price—what is known as "carbon leakage."

The EU is about to begin a new carbon policy that deals with problem.[8] Foreign firms that export to the EU will be required to purchase the same carbon permits for each ton of CO_2 associated with those products, essentially a tax or tariff based on carbon emissions. To avoid double taxation, goods imported into the EU from countries that have carbon-pricing regimes similar to the EU's will be exempt.

The carbon border tax is a step toward dealing with the international dimension of climate change. Countries that are slow to limit emissions through their domestic policies cannot avoid a carbon price if they trade with countries with a border tax. For example, China, India, and especially Russia have historically sold iron and steel to the EU. Under the border tax, the price of these imported products would rise: 17% for goods from China, 32% from India, and 26% from Russia. A weakness of this approach is that it ignores the fairness question as it punishes emitters who are in developing countries that were not major contributors to global warming in the past.

Uncertainties and Optimal Climate Policy

As one can easily imagine, there are significant uncertainties about climate change. Part of the uncertainty is based on the geophysical links between emissions, temperature change, and how temperature change affects the climate. Another source of uncertainty stems from the future path of economic production and from the evolution of energy technologies used in production that combine to determine future emissions.

Models of climate change and its effects have both geophysical and economic components. This allows researchers to consider changes in model parameters around the best available estimates to examine a range of possible outcomes. Nordhaus (2018) examines parameter uncertainty and finds that uncertainty about the rate of economic growth has the greatest impact on the range of future outcomes from climate change. While useful, this approach to uncertainty is incomplete because it does not account for unknown "tipping points" in our climate system that result in rapid and dramatic changes in temperature.

The analysis also does not include climate change effects on economic growth *rates*. An implicit assumption in the modeling of the economic effects of climate change is that the effects lower the *level* of output but not its long-run growth *rate*.[9] Future economic growth rates are perhaps the most important source of uncertainty

---

[8] See Figures et al. (2021) for a summary of the policy.

[9] This point is made by Wagner and Weitzman (2015, pp. 63–64).

about the path of climate change. The uncertainty becomes greater if climate change itself had a feedback effect on long-run growth.

How could this feedback happen? One of the key sources of economic growth is the growth in the accumulated knowledge and skills of the workforce, what economists call human capital. One of the most important factors that cause human capital and labor productivity to grow are improvements in the health and education of children (as we discuss in Chap. 3). Climate change could easily compromise the accumulation of human capital in children. Take India, a country already experiencing more dramatic heat waves associated with climate change. India is susceptible to the heat waves because it lacks clean water sources and electricity that provides air conditioning in homes and schools.[10] Excessive heat makes the health environment worse and makes learning in stifling classrooms more difficult, thereby stunting the growth in the human capital of children and productivity of its future workforce. Uncertainty over climate change and economic growth could easily be compounded through this type of interaction.

There is evidence that, in general, people are averse to risk and prefer sure things to variable outcomes with the same expected payoff. People may be particularly averse to losing something they once had (Thaler 2015). This means that people are willing to pay a significant amount for insurance against large losses of their existing property and living standards. The uncertainties associated with climate change suggest that the policy response to global warming should be aggressive in order to provide some *insurance* against the possibility of quite large losses if temperature rises toward the upper range of estimates or has more dramatic effects on the climate and the economy.

Climate R&D

In Chap. 2, we argued that basic knowledge is a public good that justifies government subsidy of basic research. Even if governments become more aggressive in pricing carbon emissions, there would still not be sufficient incentive for private innovation in brand new low-energy technologies. A high carbon price would encourage more production and use of existing low-energy technologies or even small developments in them but not riskier investments in entirely different approaches and ideas. Subsidizing research in new clean energy approaches, not in producing or tweaking existing technologies, should be part of a two-pronged climate policy.

A two-pronged climate policy, relying on *both* carbon pricing and climate R&D, is the most efficient approach governments can take. However, it must confront the political economy of climate policy. Climate policy has been painfully slow to develop. This could be because of the free rider problem. It could also be that,

[10] See, for example, Spindle (2022) and Parkin (2022).

despite polls suggesting that the majority of voters think the government should move more aggressively on climate change, they do not want to bear the burden in terms of higher energy prices. It may be that a coordinated agreement to shift the *existing* tax revenue currently used to support basic research toward research on new clean energy technology is the most politically acceptable approach to climate policy.

Climate Policy in Practice

Climate warnings and international pledges of commitment to limiting temperature increases have been around for 30 years. Efforts to focus attention on global warming has resulted in some limited climate policy action.[11] As mentioned above, at the supranational level, the EU has introduced a tradable emissions permit system. At the national level, 45 countries have attempted to price carbon, mostly through a permit system but also in some cases using a carbon tax (e.g., Canada and Sweden). At the subnational level, states, such as California, have their own permit systems. However, despite knowing that we won't make progress without a *global* policy, global carbon pricing policies are rare. Even in places with carbon pricing policies, either the price is set too low (permits are too cheap and plentiful) or the emissions covered are too narrow (only particular industries are required to participate).

In 2019, the World Bank estimated that the average price of carbon globally was only $2 per ton. This is a far cry from what is needed to meet the pledges of limiting temperature rise to 2.0 °C by the end of the century or achieving net zero emissions by 2050. To meet these types of goals, the common global price of carbon would need to be more like $100 per ton, applied to *all* possible emission sources in the world. The USA recently pledged to cut its emissions in half by 2030. It is estimated that this would require a $50 per ton price of carbon. The USA remains one of the many countries without a national carbon pricing policy. While polls suggest the majority of US voters believe the government should take steps to prevent climate change, we still have no national climate policy.

The USA does not have a national carbon policy, but many of its products are produced in a *relatively* clean manner, at least compared to other producers across the world. This happened largely for two reasons. First, the Clean Air Act of 1970 limited sulfur emissions. The use of coal as an energy source causes not only carbon emissions but sulfur as well. The Environmental Protection Agency (EPA) was charged with measuring and limiting sulfur emissions from power plants and, in addition, carbon emissions from motor vehicles and airplanes. These actions have established standards that limited our carbon emissions. Thus, the goal of improving

[11] Tirole (2017), Patnaik and Kennedy (2021), and Nordhaus (2021) contain description of current climate policy actions.

air quality has indirectly helped to limit carbon emissions in the USA. Recently, the EPA has attempted to use a broad interpretation of previous acts, such as the Clean Air Act, to move more aggressively on carbon policies such as instituting a cap-and-trade system and mandating the use of clean energy plants. A Supreme Court ruling has blocked this approach, insisting that national carbon policies of these magnitudes must be explicitly put into new laws approved by Congress. The second, and more important, reason for the decline in US carbon emissions is due to the decline in the cost of using natural gas as an energy source and, to a lesser extent, the decline in the cost of wind and solar energy as well. The laissez faire profit motive itself has played some role in reducing carbon emissions.

There are some signs of change among some US politicians as recent severe weather events are being linked in people's minds to climate change—heavy storms in the South, flooding on the East coast, and wildfires and increased ocean acidity on the West coast. However, there are key members of even the Democratic party that oppose a carbon tax and subsidies for clean energy.[12] Moderate Democrats and some Republicans have shown more enthusiasm for the a US carbon *border* tax.[13] The 2022 Inflation Reduction Act displayed concern for climate change by at least providing tax credits for clean energy investments.

The USA lacks a domestic carbon pricing policy, but it produces many goods using cleaner technologies than some of our trading partners, particularly China, India, Russia, and smaller developing countries. A border carbon "tariff" levied on emerging and developing countries has popular appeal, especially if it is not called a "tax."

Countries do have reasons to act unilaterally to limit climate change. In some cases, limiting fossil fuel consumption reduces air pollution and water shortages within the country. In other cases, there is the geopolitical advantage of not having to rely so much on countries rich in fossil fuels that have unacceptable policies in general. Finally, climate change is now starting to impose costs that are felt within most countries. Ideally, a climate policy push would come from binding international agreements. We may have to be satisfied with a more piecemeal, country-by-country approach for some time. However, even unilateral actions will have international consequences that make real progress difficult without negotiation.

Fairness and equity considerations are perhaps as much of a hurdle as the free rider problem in reaching international agreements. This was evident in recent UN climate policy discussions.[14] Large developing countries are the biggest current emitters of greenhouse gases. They need to take climate actions for the sake of the world's future. This will be costly to their economic development. They are also already facing climate problems that were primarily the result of the accumulation of past emissions from the *currently developed* countries. Developing countries are

---

[12] Davenport and Broadwater (2021).

[13] Natter, A., Wasson, E., and Dennis, S., 2022, "Manchin Eyes Tax on Carbon-Intensive Imports in Energy Package," *Bloomberg*, May 2.

[14] Hodgson and Politi (2022).

demanding financial aid from richer countries to compensate them for both the cost of taking climate action during their development stage, something the developed world did not have to do, and the damages they are currently confronting due to climate change. Richer countries have promised such aid but have not yet delivered and are defensive about making payments for current damages that they may have contributed to. This debate dominated the recent UN climate meeting and is a topic that must be dealt with to make real progress.

You can bet that developing countries that trade with richer countries, such as the EU, will not be happy about the new carbon border tax. The carbon border tax will only work with cooperation from countries exporting their goods to the EU because they will play a role in measuring the carbon intensity of their products. In addition, they will have to restrain themselves from levying retaliatory tariffs on the cleaner products imported from richer countries if the attempt to make dirty goods relatively more expensive worldwide is going to work.

The Climate Crisis and the Fiscal Crisis

The problem of climate change and the likelihood of a prompt policy response to it bears some resemblance to the fiscal crisis. Both problems have been a long time in the making: decades of greenhouse gas accumulation for climate change and decades of population aging and expanded transfer payments to retirees for the fiscal crisis. The necessary policy responses will be costly, creating an incentive for politicians and the public to ignore the problems. Ignoring the problems means their burden will be felt mostly by young and unborn generations. Inaction also increases the chance of sudden and dramatic increases in their social costs, stemming from "tipping point" and "crisis of confidence" effects when temperature change and government debt ratios exceed looming but uncertain thresholds. There is an important international dimension at play in both cases. International cooperation is crucial in lowering the shared cost of slowing global warming and the limits of continued international lending to the USA will determine the timing of the fiscal crisis fallout.

As mentioned in Chap. 2, the problems are related in another way. Imposing a significant carbon tax will discourage activities that cause greenhouse gas accumulation and encourage the development and use of cleaner energy sources. In addition, the revenue collected from the carbon tax is an economically efficient step toward reducing government budget deficits.

What Should (Can) the USA Do?

Earlier in this century, it seemed likely that the fiscal crisis would be the first problem to impose severe and transparent costs on our economy in the form of higher real interest rates and perhaps a financial crisis. Yet the fiscal crisis is not a serious issue in US political discussion. The world demand for US government debt has kept pace with the growing supply, and real interests in global credit markets, while higher, remain low enough not to create panic over debt servicing costs. Instead, climate change is now the problem with transparent costs. If the timing had been the opposite, it would have been easier to pass a carbon tax policy as an efficient way to collect more tax revenue to address the fiscal crisis. Currently a carbon tax, or any form of domestic carbon pricing, remains a non-starter politically at the national level in the USA.

The best we can probably do right now is pursue the idea of a border carbon tax. Another possibility is to propose a domestic carbon tax where the tax burden is offset by lowering income tax rates. This approach is supported by the literature on the MCPF, may be acceptable politically, and at least would not worsen the fiscal situation.

Placing a priority on climate change by shifting available funding for basic research toward the development of new clean technologies might also be possible. Additional government spending on subsidies for existing solar and wind technologies and electric vehicles worsens the fiscal crisis. It also faces opposition from our allies who believe it undermines free trade principles because it favors US production over foreign production. Shifting *existing* basic research funding toward research relevant to climate change would not worsen the fiscal situation, would not face political opposition because it does not pose an immediate threat to domestic coal and natural gas industries, and would not violate trade agreements.

The USA is lagging other rich countries in government policy actions to address climate change. Taking modest domestic steps will create political leverage to push forward international climate change discussions with our allies and the rest of the world. The potential of climate change agreements will also be enhanced by more effective policies of development aid and continued attention to free trade principles.

References

Bannister, G., and Mourmouras, A., 2017, "Welfare vs Income Convergence and Environmental Externalities," IMF Working Paper No. 17/271, International Monetary Fund: Washington DC.

Boadway, R., and Wildasin, D., 1984, *Public Sector Economics*, Boston: Little, Brown and Company.

Bovenberg, A., and Goulder, L, 1996, "Optimal Environmental Taxation in the Presence of Other Taxes: General Equilibrium Analyses," *American Economic Review*, 86, 985–1000.

Climate Action Tracker (2021), "Warming Projections Global Update," November, Berlin: Climate Analytics Institute.

Davenport, C. and Broadwater, L., 2021, "Democrats Weigh Carbon Tax after Manchin Rejects Key Climate Provisions," *New York Times*, October 16.

Figures, T., Gilbert, M., McAdoo, M., and Voigt, N., 2021, "The EU's Carbon Border Tax will Redefine Global Value Chains," *BCG Publications*, www.bcg.com.

Hausfather, Z., 2021, "Global CO2 Emissions have been Flat for a Decade, New Data Reveals," *Carbon Brief*, November 11.

Hodgson, C., and Politi, J., 2022, "UN Climate Talks end in Acrimony and Accusations of Betrayal," *Financial Times*, June 17.

Ivanyna, M, and Mourmouras, A., 2023, "Beyond GDP: Welfare Around the World with Environmental and Sustainability Adjustments," *IMF Working Paper*, (forthcoming).

Lange, G.M., Wodon, Q., and Carey, K., 2018, *The Changing Wealth of Nations*, Washington D.C.: The World Bank Group.

McKitrick, R., 2016, "A Practical Guide to the Economics of Carbon Pricing," *The School of Public Policy Research Papers*, Volume 9 Issue 28, University of Calgary.

Natter, A., Wasson, E., and Dennis, S., 2022, "Manchin Eyes Tax on Carbon-Intensive Imports in Energy Package," *Bloomberg*, May 2.

Nordhaus, W., 2013, *The Climate Casino*, New Haven: Yale University Press.

———., 2018, "Projections and Uncertainties about Climate Change in an Era of Minimal Climate Policies," *American Economic Journal: Economic Policy*, 10(3), 333–360

———., 2021, "Why Climate Policy Has Failed," *Foreign Affairs*, October 12.

Parkin, B., 2022, "Delhi's Heatwaves Carry a Warning for the Rest of the World," *Financial Times*.

Patnaik, S., and Kennedy, K., 2021, "Why the US Should Establish a Carbon Price either through Reconciliation or other Legislation," *Brookings Report*, October 7

Ritchie, H., Roser, M., and Rosado, P., 2020, "CO2 and Greenhouse Emissions," Published Online at OurWorldData.org

Spindle, B., 2022, "On the Grid in Leisang," *New York Review*, June 22.

Stern, N., 2006, *The Economics of Climate Change: The Stern Review*, Cambridge: Cambridge University Press.

Thaler, R., 2015, *Misbehaving,* New York: W.W. Norton and Company.

Tirole, J., 2017, *Economics for the Common Good*, Princeton: Princeton University Press.

Wagner, G,, and Weitzman, M., 2015, *Climate Shock*, Princeton: Princeton University Press.

Chapter 6
Policy Reforms Summary

This final chapter summarizes the suggested policy reforms that are supported by economic research. We start by noting that policy failures are a major reason for the problems the USA faces in the twenty-first century. These policy failures are similar to those made by leading countries in the past. The difficulty of establishing and maintaining good governance has always been with us, driven throughout history by a common set of human characteristics. The challenge of enduring success is to first recognize these human failings and then create institutions that provide the needed checks on our behavior. Next, we review the specific sources of each of our major economic challenges. Finally, the reforms needed to address each challenge are stated with an eye to their overall consistency and coordination.

Is Government Failure Inevitable?

Government leadership in creating public capital, laws, and services that facilitate private enterprise is necessary to initiate and sustain growth. In many societies around the world, the public interest that motivates good governance is dominated by the private interests of those in power to such an extent that modern sustained growth is never achieved. Perhaps more difficult to understand is why governments, which at one time *did* provide the necessary leadership, begin to fail, contributing to an economic growth slowdown that prevents successful societies from progressing.

The issue of government failure is connected to the broader question of why successful societies slip back, often quite dramatically. There are general theories of decline that claim failure is inevitable—fundamental flaws in human nature interact with success in a way that leads to a reversal of fortune.[1] Government failure in

[1] See a survey of those theories by Ophlus (2012).

© The Author(s), under exclusive license to Springer Nature Switzerland AG 2023

A. Mourmouras, P. Rangazas, *US Economic Policy in the 21st Century*, Professional Practice in Governance and Public Organizations,
https://doi.org/10.1007/978-3-031-36437-2_6

successful societies can be thought of as a reflection of these underlying fundamental flaws. Why can't we learn from past failures and use the government to help discipline human weakness?

There are reasons for growth slowdowns that are independent of human behavior per se. Limits in resources and human abilities create diminishing returns to investment in physical and human capital—a basic assumption of economic analysis. But how societies respond to diminishing returns determines *how much* growth declines. Humans are hardwired, from their long evolution as hunter-gathers, to survive day-to-day. This causes us to focus much more on the present than the future. The recent research in behavioral economics argues the pull of present consumption is so strong it causes us to behave "irrationally." We save and exercise less, and smoke and eat more, than we really want to.[2] Diminishing returns, which weaken the payoffs to investment, nudge us toward our natural instincts to consume at high rates.

The accumulated wealth from past investments also naturally causes hunter-gathers to conserve energy by focusing on easy pickings. Why not become better-off by arguing that we deserve a bigger share of all this wealth? The existing wealth of rich societies creates its own force to favor redistribution over production, similar to the natural resource curse that plagues some developing countries. A growing sense of entitlement causes the proliferation of interest groups in successful societies, as noted by Olsen (1982). The proliferation of interest groups creates factions that compete for the nation's wealth. Again, the situation resembles that in poor countries that fail to develop because of factious conflict that undermines the national interest needed to form pro-growth policies. Weak national interest gives way to group politics, a problem that can affect growth at the earliest and latest stages of development.[3]

The interest groups in the rich countries of the twentieth century began asking more of government to make life easier, safer, and fairer. The well-intended response of governments is to create more laws and provide more transfers and services—serving to promote rents over growth. This trend leads to another one of the general sources of decline in successful societies—growing complexity. Complexity is the enemy of the transparency needed to keep government honest. Complexity is also bad for growth because it forces societies to devote more resources to simply maintaining the system—a depreciation cost associated with large institutional capital. Growing complexity means more politicians, officials, bureaucrats, lawyers, analysts, lobbyists, and the professors needed to train them all. Complexity results in a myriad of unintended consequences such as greater costs of production, declining transparency, and growing income inequality because of an increased demand for highly skilled labor needed to maintain the system. Complexity biases investments

---

[2] See Thaler (2015) for a discussion of self-control.

[3] See Tornell and Lane (1999) and Ivanyna et al. (2021, section 3.6) for a discussion of how interest groups vying for a portion of a common pool of tax revenue drive total transfer spending up.

away from productive skills and toward rent-seeking skills, reinforcing the "wealth curse" that created the complexity to begin with.

Success also naturally leads to complacency and hubris that takes attention away from domestic improvement and undermines international relations. The citizens, especially the key decision-makers, begin to feel content and superior. The successful country becomes defensive and fails to acknowledge and address its most important shortcomings. Uncomfortable trends that do not have immediate consequences are dismissed. Overconfidence causes policymakers to believe that all problems will eventually be solved; "perhaps not now but later, when the problem really needs to be addressed." The same sense of superiority can also cause interest in and respect for other countries to wane, making mutually advantageous economic and political international exchanges more difficult.

To deal with the twenty-first-century economic challenges, the USA must shift resources toward efficient public investments, foster international economic activity, and reduce government complexity.

Economic Challenges

Slowing Long-Run Economic Growth

The first source of the growth slowdown is the diminishing returns to all types of investment—physical capital, human capital, and government capital. Some also believe that investment in research and development of new technologies is subject to diminishing returns—more recent inventions are more resource costly and lack the productivity impact of their predecessors.

Then there is the leveling and, in some cases, reduction in the *rates* of investment as countries develop. Aggregate savings rates fall and consumption rates rise, reducing funds for private capital investment. The ability of a nation to push larger fractions of the population through higher education stalls because the majority of the population lacks the aptitude and attitude to complete college. The allocation of government revenue to basic research and infrastructure investment is cut in favor of transfers programs.

In part, the reduction in investment rates may be caused by the falling rates of return that serve to lower the reward and incentive to investment. However, much of the reduction is due to government policy favoring consumption and inefficient investment. The rise in intergenerational redistribution to the elderly causes a fall in national saving, as well as a reduction in government funding available for investment. Within the portions of government budgets allocated for education, unrealistic elitism has created a bias toward higher education that has the unintended consequence of primarily benefiting the rich and widening income inequality. Too much is spent on tuition subsidies for higher education and student loans, and too little is spent on investments in young children from lower-income families and in well-designed vocational training for teenagers. More generally, politics often favor the allocation of public investment projects to richer and more powerful regions of the nation, despite the likelihood of higher rates of return in neglected communities where public capital is scarce.

Rising Income Inequality

As economies develop, there is a natural rise in the relative demand for skilled labor. A succinct description of this tendency is provided by Autor (2014, p. 845).

> A technologically advanced economy requires a literate, numerate, technically and scientifically trained workforce to develop ideas, manage complex organizations, deliver health care services, provide financing and insurance, and operate critical infrastructure. As physical labor has given way to cognitive labor, the labor markets demand for formal analytical skills, written communication, and specific technical knowledge—what economists often loosely term cognitive skills—has risen spectacularly.

The rise in the demand for skilled, highly educated workers has increased the labor market *skill premium*—the wage of skilled workers relative to unskilled workers. A higher skill premium has increased the demand for education and caused a rise in the relative price of college. In richer families, the children are well-prepared for college and the parents can afford the rising cost. Many of these children not only go to college, but also graduate—ultimately receiving high returns on their human capital investments. In households below the mean, college preparedness is poor and parents cannot afford to help much with the rising cost of tuition. For these reasons, large fractions of the population do not even attempt college and many of those that do fail to graduate.

The policies designed to push greater fractions of young people through college have failed because of a lack of investment early in children's lives and because many students, from both rich and poor families, simply do not have a taste for academics. Government education subsidies are predominately helping richer families whose children would have attended and graduated from college at high rates without subsidies.

The supply of skilled workers has not kept pace with the demand. Workers who did not graduate from college, the majority of the workforce, have few skills. These two factors have caused the skill premium to rise over time.

Furthermore, college graduates as a group have not fared well in the labor market—seeing at most modest increases in real wages for decades. The modest in the *average* wage received by graduates is connected to a rise in "residual" wage inequality, i.e., a rise in wage inequality *among* college graduates. Only students with quantitative majors or ones that receive advanced graduate degrees obtain high paying jobs. Many college graduates would be in a better economic situation if they had received quality vocational training in high school and not attended college at all.

Looming Fiscal and Financial Crises

The large unfunded government liabilities are primarily associated with the rise in government transfers to the elderly. Population aging, combined with the rise in medical costs and the PAYG financing of social programs, have generated rapidly growing intergenerational transfers.

However, this does not explain why the broad middle class is relatively comfortable with intergenerational redistribution and rising debt. Discretionary household consumption has become increasingly constrained by (i) the lack of median real income growth and (ii) the rise in the cost of required investments in health and education. Families needing to make the health and education investments that give themselves and their children a chance at a quality life have become increasingly willing to use the government to transfer the financial burden of these investments to future generations. The negative economic consequences of growing public debt have not yet been fully realized because international credit markets have provided low interest funding to high-borrowing countries such as the USA. Real interest rates have risen recently and there are indication that they could rise further.

Politics also plays a role in the fiscal crisis. Special interest groups tend to accumulate in democracies. Politicians respond to the interest groups for political support. Driven by the perverse incentives of the common pool problem, the natural political response results in more spending and a larger and more complex government where advantages and favors to special interest groups are less transparent.

Federal government spending is currently dominated by mandatory "entitlement" programs, in particular Social Security, Medicare, and Medicaid. These programs are written into law and are largely protected from the annual discussion of the discretionary components of the budget. Interest groups representing the elderly, the medical profession, drug companies, and the poor have rewarded politicians with support because of their protection and expansion of entitlement programs. The fiscal crisis is worsened by the "tax expenditures" that politicians give out in the form of tax allowances and deductions to interest groups that include homeowners, firms that provide health insurance, and rich asset holders.

The frustration of the middle class has likely contributed to the increased polarization of politics that makes it difficult to reconcile the financial inconsistency of the government's policies. The result is a growing gap between spending and tax collection summarized by the fiscal gap.

Geopolitical Tensions

Most analysts predict a retrenchment of globalization. Russia's aggression and the pandemic are life-altering events that made many think seriously about the value of international connections. However, before these dramatic events, there was already significant pushback against globalization. The pushback stemmed from economic frustration and knee-jerk scapegoating. The growth slowdown, the rise in inequality, and the persistent dependence of the USA on foreign saving that causes the trade deficit all led to the misguided populist movement against international trade, capital mobility, and immigration. In fact, the evidence indicates that the USA benefits from globalization. Reforms of US policies, mostly domestic, would increase those benefits.

Climate Change

The warming of the planet due to the carbon emissions associated with economic activity will have significant and potentially devastating consequences. Current economic challenges have made it difficult for societies to focus attention on the future costs of climate change, similar to the reason the USA is not addressing the fiscal crisis. While both the fiscal crisis and climate change are neglected because needed policy reforms involve immediate pain in exchange for future benefits, climate change policy is fundamentally harder. Fiscal reform is a domestic issue. Climate change policy reform must involve international cooperation and coordination.

Policy Reforms

Step 1: Human Capital Reforms

The persistent fiscal gap, the inability to limit climate change, and the resistance to globalization are partly due to economic frustration. Most US households recognize that debt, global warming, and economic isolation threaten the welfare of their children. However, most US households are already struggling to match the living standards of their parent's generation. A 4-year college education in a well-chosen major is a good investment for a relatively small portion of each age cohort. Too many young people are not as productive as they should be, unable to afford a satisfying lifestyle going forward.

Before people will accept the sacrifices needed to address our twenty-first-century problems, they and their children must first become more productive and make better livings. Shifting our education investment toward preschool learning and vocational training in high school offers a well-documented way to raise productivity and reduce inequality. The reduced economic frustration will allow more serious consideration of the other reforms.

Beyond the microeconomic evidence supporting the high potential returns of US vocational education investments (provided in Chap. 3), cross-country macroeconomic evidence is consistent with the idea that a shift toward vocational education could pay off quickly in terms of higher economic growth. Germany is noted for their focus on vocational education. This is a possible explanation for why total factor productivity growth in German manufacturing has far outpaced that in the USA during the twenty-first century. Bailey et al. (2020) estimate that from 2004 to 2016, TFP growth in the manufacturing sector was 1.9% in Germany and only 0.7% in the USA. In fact, the authors hypothesize that its superior productivity growth could be because Germany invests much more in workforce training.

All reforms must confront the reality of the long-term federal shortfall in revenues. The federal government currently spends about the same as states on student and public university subsidies to higher education. Pell Grants, the G.I. Bill, and tax expenditures to families with higher education costs amounted to about $80 billion in 2017–2018 (Stauffer 2019). This federal funding should be shifted to support preschool and high school vocational initiatives at the state level. Over a 10-year period, the tax expenditures should be eliminated and the merit standards for receiving Pell and G.I. funding should be dramatically strengthened to free funds without the need for more government borrowing.

Step 2: Resist De-Globalization

International economic policy offers an opportunity to increase economic growth before fiscal consolidation. Geopolitical tensions are causing reduced trade with China and Russia. For the sake of maintaining working relations with these two large economies, some level of trade with them should be continued. To offset the loss of trade with China and Russia, trade agreements with US allies should move closer to a free trade position. The Infrastructure Investment and Jobs Act and the education reforms suggested above will allow more US workers to benefit from capital mobility, as better infrastructure and a more productive middle-skills workforce attract multinationals to set up operations in the USA. Finally, legal immigration must be made easier. Not only for high-skilled labor as suggested by Alden (2022) and Wadhwa (2012), but for workers at all skill levels. Immigrants are disproportionately linked to new business formation and patents. Greater immigration will also balance the USA demographically, increasing the portion of the population that is working and paying taxes.

Step 3: Fiscal Consolidation and Climate Policy

Following the first two steps will create a more prosperous economic environment across the income spectrum, making for a public that should be more willing to confront the fiscal crisis and climate change. The suggestions on fiscal consolidation from Chap. 2 are stated again here with one addition that also addresses climate change.

1. Increase the age at which the minimum and maximum Social Security retirement benefits are received.
2. Reduce Social Security benefit levels for higher income individuals.
3. Cap expenditures under Medicare and Medicaid, at the current percentage of GDP, by offering a basic plan of healthcare coverage that is revised annually by a healthcare panel.
4. Increase tax revenue by investing in tax compliance and eliminating tax expenditures starting with the tax exclusion for the health insurance provided as a worker benefit, the reduced tax rate on income from capital gains, and the deductibility of mortgage interest on owner-occupied housing.
5. Increase tax revenue by increasing a variety of Pigovian taxes, sin taxes, and a federal sales tax.
6. Increase budgets for public infrastructure (even after the Infrastructure Investment and Jobs Act there is more to be done here) and basic research (for which nothing has been done).
7. For the purpose of minimizing negative effects on output in the short run, consolidation packages should tend to favor spending cuts over tax increases in reducing the fiscal gap.
8. Impose a carbon tax. The carbon tax contribution to solving both the fiscal crisis and climate change makes so much sense that it will eventually win majority support in the country. Carbon taxation done right requires difficult international coordination. This is a major reason that we must strengthen international alliances with our allies and continue to trade and talk with Russia and China.

Our allies have objected strongly to our government subsidies for clean energy production in the Inflation Reduction Act. Chinese government subsidies to its industries are a common target by the USA when we complain about non-tariff policies that deviate from free trade by creating an "unlevel playing field." Government subsidies that encourage the transition to clean energy are acceptable under international trade agreements, but there are objections when subsidies are tied to the use of clean energy *production only in the USA*. For example, it may be to receive subsidies for the use of wind turbines or electric vehicles, they must be produced in the USA. It is likely that we need to back off these US production only subsidies in negotiations with allies. Instead, in addition to imposing a carbon tax, it may be more politically feasible for governments to jointly agree to increase shared support for *basic research* toward the development of new clean technologies and products without directing where the factories producing the new products will be located.

Emergency Actions

A bond market reaction similar to the one experienced by the UK in 2022 could happen in the USA just as suddenly if circumstances cause a sharp increase in the government budget deficit. In addition, Medicare is very close to being illiquid, it is already insolvent, in the sense that annual payroll tax revenue will soon fall short of the promised annual benefit payout. This shortfall is now expected within the next 5 years but the exact date changes because the payroll tax base can increase or decrease unexpectedly. Annual Social Security funding shortfalls are projected to occur soon after those facing Medicare.

These events will force the government to move fast, demonstrating to financial markets that policy changes are being made to address the situation, with a strong signal that more substantial reforms will follow. What reasonable and quick policy changes could be made without worsening economic growth or wage inequality? Below are six possible reforms: two that would raise tax revenue directly, two that would increase the tax base, and two that would limit spending. All of these have been defended previously, along with other reforms, and have been chosen because we think they might be expedient ways of dealing with a crisis.

Changes in Tax Policy

The largest US tax expenditure is the exclusion of taxes on employer benefits paid in the form of health insurance. There is nothing good about this policy that was created as a quick fix to get around another bad policy—wage and price controls during WWII. The policy creates allocative inefficiencies and is regressive. Taxing these benefits as just another form of wages would raise about $300 billion in income and payroll tax revenue. A fiscal emergency would also be an opportunity to introduce, at least, a small carbon tax that would get us going down a road we need to eventually follow. Offering a carbon tax as a substitute for other tax increases proposed in a time of crisis should increase the likelihood of passing this important legislation.

Raising the Tax Base

One of the quickest ways to raise economic growth and increase the income and payroll tax base is to make legal immigration easier for workers at all skill levels. Expand the cap on H1-B visas. An improved immigration system would also help with the US border problem, an issue that the majority of citizens want the government to address. Another way to raise economic growth relatively quickly is to reallocate education expenditures away from college, by increasing the merit standard for receiving federal government support for college, and toward vocational programs. Investment in vocational education is no more important than investment in preschools, but it has the advantage of raising the skills of the workforce more quickly.

Cutting Government Spending

The best quick-and-dirty way to limit spending under Medicare is simply to have the government cover a smaller portion of all medical services and treatments across the board. Yes, this is a temporary "default" on Medicare obligations, the burden of which will be shared by private insurance, individuals, and medical professionals. Capping Medicare coverage is an absolute necessity to resolve the long-term fiscal crisis. The temporary reduction in coverage should be just enough to balance annual outlay with payroll tax inflows until a better reform is formulated. An across-the-board cut in discretionary spending should also be imposed (cuts to other programs under the Department of Education should be disproportionately larger so as to protect the funding reallocated to vocational education).

References

Alden, E., 2022, "Immigration has Become an Elaborate Bait and Switch," *Foreign Policy*, October 27.

Autor, D., 2014, "Skills, Education, and the Rise in Earnings Inequality among the Other 99 Percent," *Science*, 344, 843–851.

Bailey, N., Bosworth, B., and Doshi, S., 2020, "Productivity Comparisons: Lessons from Japan, the United States, and Germany," *Economic Studies at Brookings*, Washington DC: Brookings Institution.

Ivanyna, M., Mourmouras, A., and Rangazas, P., 2021, *The Macroeconomics of Corruption*, New York: Springer.

Olsen, M., 1982, *The Rise and Decline of Nations: Economic Growth, Stagflation, and Social Rigidities*, New Haven: Yale university Press.

Ophlus, W., 2012, *Immoderate Greatness*, Charleston: Create Space Independent Publishing.

Stauffer, A., 2019, "Two Decades of Change in Federal and State Higher Education Funding," PEW Charitable Trust.

Thaler, R., 2015, *Misbehaving: The Making of Behavioral Economics*, New York: W.W. Norton

Tornell, A., and Lane, P., 1999, "The Voracity Effect," *American Economic Review*, 89, 22–46.

Wadhwa, V., 2012, *The Immigration Exodus*, Philadelphia: Warton Digital Press.

Index

© The Editor(s) (if applicable) and The Author(s), under exclusive license to Springer Nature Switzerland AG 2023

A. Mourmouras, P. Rangazas, *US Economic Policy in the 21st Century*, Professional Practice in Governance and Public Organizations,
https://doi.org/10.1007/978-3-031-36437-2